Reading Shakespeare Today

MACBETH

Katie Griffiths

Cavendish Square
New York

Published in 2016 by Cavendish Square Publishing, LLC
243 5th Avenue, Suite 136, New York, NY 10016

First Edition

Cataloging-in-Publication Data

Griffiths, Katie.
Macbeth / by Katie Griffiths.
p. cm. — (Reading Shakespeare today)
Includes index.
ISBN 978-1-5026-1041-6 (hardcover) ISBN 978-1-5026-1042-3 (e-book)
1. Shakespeare, William, — 1564-1616. — Macbeth — Juvenile literature. I. Griffiths, Katie. II. Title.
PR2823.G75 2016
822.3'3—d23

Editorial Director: David McNamara
Editor: Andrew Coddington
Copy Editor: Rebecca Rohan
Art Director: Jeffrey Talbot
Designer: Stephanie Flecha
Senior Production Manager: Jennifer Ryder-Talbot
Production Editor: Renni Johnson
Photo Research: J8 Media

The photographs in this book are used by permission and through the courtesy of: Ron Scherl/Redferns/Getty, cover; Shutterstock, cover and throughout the book; PHAS/Prisma/UIG/ Getty Images, 5; By Schlaier (Own work) [Public domain], via Wikimedia Commons, 6; By unknown, English School (http://www.philipmould.com/zoom.php? sid=2454&p=sa) [Public domain], via Wikimedia Commons, 9; Jack Vartoogian/Getty Images, 11; Culture Club/Getty Images, 13; See page for author [CC BY 4.0 (http://creativecommons.org/licenses/by/4.0)], via Wikimedia Commons, 15; By William Creswell from Seattle, Washington, USA (Lady Macbeth) [Public domain or CC BY 2.0 (http://creativecommons.org/licenses/by/2.0)], via Wikimedia Commons, 17; Photo by REX/Newscom, 22; Hiroyuki Ito/Getty Images, 24; Duncan's Horses, 1842 (oil on canvas), John Frederick Herring, Sr.(1795-1865)/Private Collection/Christie's Images/Bridgeman Images, 29; Hiroyuki Ito/Getty Images, 34; DeAgostini/Getty Images, 37; Macbeth and the Apparition of the Armed Head, Act IV, Scene I, from 'Macbeth', by William Shakespeare (1564-1616) c.1820 (w/c, wash, pen & ink on paper), Craig, William Marshall (fl.1788- 1828)/Yale Center for British Art, Paul Mellon Collection, USA/Bridgeman Images, 39; AP Photo/Chris Miller, 42; Lady Macbeth Sleepwalking, illustration from 'Macbeth' by William Shakespeare (1564-1616) c.1900 (litho), Scheiner, Artus (1863-1938)/Private Collection/ Archives Charmet/Bridgeman Images, 46; John Martin [Public domain], via Wikimedia Commons, 48; Hulton Archive/Getty Images, 50; Mr Alexander as Macduff, and Mr Irving as Macbeth (gravure), English School, (19th century) / Private Collection/ Look and Learn/Bridgeman Images, 52; Hulton Archive/Getty Images, 53; Chris Ball/Evening Standard/Hulton Archive/Getty Images, 55; Alastair Muir/REX/Newscom, 57; Frank Herrmann NI Syndication/Newscom, 61; Universal History Archive/UIG via Getty Images, 67; Art Media/Print Collector/Getty Images, 69; Popperfoto/Getty Images, 71; By R. W. Billings [Public domain], via Wikimedia Commons, 74; by Ester Inbar, available from http://commons.wikimedia.org/wiki/User:ST. [Attribution], via Wikimedia Commons, 77; Keystone/Getty Images, 86.

Printed in the United States of America

CONTENTS

Introduction

SHAKESPEARE AND HIS WORLD

William Shakespeare casts a long shadow. Since the Elizabethan age, he has been widely seen as one of the greatest English playwrights who ever lived. He wrote dozens of plays, and volumes of poetry. His words have been passed down through the generations, sometimes without us even knowing whom we are quoting. He has created characters that are still recognized and relatable today, from the philosophical Hamlet, to the ambitious Lady Macbeth, to the passionate Romeo. But who is this man? And why do we keep returning to his work?

Mystery surrounds Shakespeare's life. Despite scholars' continued interest in him, very little is known for certain. This is largely because few records were kept during his time. It is believed that Shakespeare was born in the town of Stratford-upon-Avon in the country of Warwickshire, England, in April 1564. He was baptized on April 26 of that year. He was one of several children in the Shakespeare family, though most of his brothers and sisters died young. In 1582, when he was eighteen, he married Anne Hathaway, who was eight years his senior. They had three children: Susanna, Hamnet, and Judith. From the early 1590s, William was a member of London's leading acting company,

The Bard himself, William Shakespeare

Shakespeare's Globe Theatre burned down in 1613 when a prop cannon set fire to the thatched roof. A modern-day reproduction was opened in 1997, just 750 feet (229 m) from the site of the original.

The Lord Chamberlain's Men. He first found fame with his 1593 poem, *Venus and Adonis*.

During this period, theaters were more primitive. There was no indoor lighting so plays could only be performed outdoors in the afternoon. Most theaters were set up like enclosed courtyards with open roofs. Poor people stood on the ground in front of the stage, while wealthier people sat in covered, raised tiers above. There were few props or special effects and almost no scenery. Whole battles were represented by just a few actors, and ghosts or witches would "magically" appear though a trapdoor in the stage floor. In addition, actors would have to deal with rowdy audiences. There was no such thing as sitting quietly through a performance. The people were there to be entertained and would make sure the actors knew if they weren't doing their job properly!

At first glance, Shakespeare's world was very different from ours. With no phones or Internet, communication was slow, and most poor people could not read. Life expectancy was also much shorter, most children died young, and starvation was common. Under these harsh conditions, entertainment was a luxury that few could afford. As a result, actors and musicians were in constant competition to attract spectators and their meager incomes. Shakespeare was very aware of this. He wrote plays to reflect his volatile times. However, he also chose themes that were immortal and universal—love, family, ambition, fear. His limited resources forced him instead to focus on ideas that could be easily understood by all classes of society. Instead of complicated props and effects, he used the beauty of language to convey pain and joy. It is his words that we return to time and again, because they express our own humanity.

Chapter One

Shakespeare and *Macbeth*

James I of England had been James VI of Scotland for twenty years before becoming king of England. Shakespeare wrote *Macbeth* in 1606 to honor James and his Scottish ancestry. He discovered the story in *Holinshed's Chronicles*, a popular contemporary history book that was also a source for a number of Shakespeare's other plays. However, Shakespeare made some changes in the history to suit his own purposes. For example, he made King Duncan old and venerable instead of young and weak. He also, for good reason, presented Macbeth's friend Banquo as honorable when he was originally part of the plan to kill Duncan. The real Banquo was the founder of the Stuart line, from which James I descended. Glorifying Banquo and creating a scene where a long line of Banquo's descendants appear in one of Macbeth's hallucinations supported James's fantasy that his descendants would "rule over Britain to the end of the world."

Shakespeare reserved his biggest changes, however, for the character of Macbeth. In *Holinshed*, Macbeth is a one-dimensional warrior-type who served as king of Scotland for ten years. He's no shrinking violet in *Macbeth*, but he is capable of degrees of self-reflection, guilt, and remorse that the real-life ruler probably never displayed. Even though we may feel sympathy for Macbeth, however, the play must have made a tremendous impact at the royal court for another reason. Only a year before its first performance, James's life had been endangered by the Gunpowder Plot, a failed attempt by Guy Fawkes and others to blow up Parliament and the king at Parliament's opening ceremony in 1605.

King James I of England, also known as James VI of Scotland

Shakespeare also engaged the interests of James in another way: the Weird Sisters. James was a great believer in and a respected authority on witches; he even wrote about witchcraft in his book *Daemonologie* (1599).

Shakespeare at the Movies

IT IS HARDLY surprising that Macbeth has been adapted many times for the silver screen. Its study of power, ambition, and human frailty are such universal themes that *Macbeth* could be shown and understood almost anywhere. And indeed, the play has traveled and been transmuted through many different settings and times. Some of its most popular screen adaptations include:

Kumonosu-jo (1957)

Known in English as *Throne of Blood*, this Japanese film was directed by the renowned filmmaker Akira Kurosawa. He directed other famous Japanese films such as *Seven Samurai* (1954) and *Ran* (1985). He moves *Macbeth* to feudal Japan and transforms the title character into General Washizu, a samurai warrior. He introduces new elements, such as using evil spirits instead of the three Weird Sisters, and places Washizu in further confusion by making Lady Washizu fall pregnant shortly after they kill the Lord (who plays the character of Duncan).

Macbeth (1971)

This Roman Polanski film is one of the Western world's most famous Shakespearean screen adaptations. Filmed shortly after the murder of Polanski's wife, Sharon Tate, it is characterized by extreme

Washizu and Lady Asaji in *Throne of Blood*

pessimism and violence. Polanski claimed he wanted to "show [*Macbeth's*] violence the way it is … [because] if you don't show it realistically then that's immoral and harmful." He even added an epilogue that shows Donalbain, Malcolm's brother, arriving at the witches' lair, indicating that the cycle of violence will begin again.

Macbeth (2006)

Macbeth's most recent film adaptation is set in modern-day Melbourne, Australia, amongst a criminal gang. Macbeth is now an underboss to the crime boss Duncan, who is given a prophecy by a group of teenage schoolgirl witches. Drugs and alcohol feature largely, providing explanation for Macbeth's increasingly unhinged mental state. The script still largely maintains the language of the original play.

Chapter Two

The Play's the Thing

Act I, Scene 1

Overview

It is a dark and stormy night on a Scottish moor. Three witches appear and plan to meet Macbeth after he's defeated his king's enemies in battle.

Analysis

What an opening! There is thunder and lightning to grab attention, and three eerie witches. In addition to being riveting, this play is also going to be dark. Practically everything in *Macbeth* happens in the dark, which the Elizabethans feared even more than children do today. Nothing good ever happened in the dark. Darkness represented evil and the unknown.

The three witches

The opening scene also mentions Graymalkin and Paddock, who are the witches' pets or "familiars." They could take the form of anything from a toad to a cat.

Act I, Scene 2

Overview

A bleeding soldier tells King Duncan and his son Malcolm how bravely Macbeth and Banquo fought against the rebel Macdonwald and his Irish supporters. Macbeth sliced Macdonwald open from his navel to his jaws, cut off his head, and put it on the Scottish battlements. No sooner is the soldier carried off than a messenger arrives with news that Macbeth has also defeated the traitorous Thane of Cawdor and his Norwegian supporters. His throne saved, King Duncan proclaims Macbeth, the Thane of Glamis, the new Thane of Cawdor.

Analysis

In the first scene we had darkness; now we have blood. Darkness and blood permeate this play. Macbeth's beheading of Macdonwald also foreshadows his own beheading by Macduff at the play's end.

Act I, Scene 3

Overview

Macbeth and Banquo meet the three Weird Sisters for the first time. When the brave soldiers appear, however, they shrink in horror at the sight of witches. Banquo says they don't look like "inhabitants of the earth."

Macbeth and Banquo meet the witches.

The witches hail Macbeth as Thane of Cawdor, which puzzles him, since he has not yet heard about his new title. The witches tell Macbeth that someday he will be king, and they inform Banquo that he won't be king but his descendants will. Before Macbeth can learn more, they disappear.

Macbeth and Banquo begin discussing the witches' strange prophecy, but they are interrupted by a messenger from Duncan. Macbeth is the new Thane of Cawdor. The witches' prophecy has come true! Macbeth asks Banquo if he hopes his children will be kings, but Banquo cautions that sometimes "instruments of darkness" tell half-truths in order to cause harm. Macbeth ignores him. He's wondering if Duncan's crown will somehow fall into his lap or if he will have to be more active. As they are about to leave the heath, Macbeth tells Banquo that they should talk about what has happened at a later time. Banquo agrees.

Analysis

In the previous scene, Macbeth was a brave warrior. However, his fascination with the witches' prophecy reveals an ambition so great he's willing to contemplate murder. Macbeth doesn't say that he will kill the king, but this thought does come readily to his mind. Some critics claim that he may have already been thinking about it.

The first words Macbeth speaks in the play, "So foul and fair a day I have not seen," echo the witches' previous statement:"Fair is foul and foul is fair." Macbeth's words underscore Banquo's warning that not everything is what it seems.

Act I, Scene 4

Overview

At the palace, Malcolm tells his father, King Duncan, that the rebellious former Thane of Cawdor has confessed to treason and been executed. When Macbeth and Banquo enter, Duncan thanks them for their service. Macbeth proclaims his loyalty to the king, and Duncan announces that his son Malcolm will be his heir. Macbeth pretends to be pleased with this news, but realizes that Malcolm now stands between him and the crown. Plans are made for everyone to dine at Macbeth's castle that evening, and Macbeth leaves ahead of the others to tell his wife to expect company.

Analysis

By opening this scene with the news of Cawdor's death, Shakespeare reminds his audience of the seriousness of the Thane's crime. When immediately afterward the audience hears Macbeth wondering what to do now that Malcolm's been named heir, they cannot help connecting Macbeth with the fate of the dead Thane. Furthermore, Cawdor's acceptance of his execution without resistance foreshadows Macbeth's resignation toward his own death.

The infamous Lady Macbeth

Act I, Scene 5

Overview

At the Macbeths' castle in Inverness, Lady Macbeth reads a letter from her husband. She learns of the prophecies and regrets that Macbeth has the ambition but not the wickedness to kill the king. His nature, she says, is too "full of the milk of human kindness." What he needs is a push.

After a messenger announces that Macbeth and Duncan are on their way, Lady Macbeth delivers her first telling lines. She begs the spirits to "unsex" her and says that if she were a man, she would kill the king herself.

Macbeth arrives. He tells his wife that Duncan plans to spend the night in their castle and she informs him that the king will never again see the sun. She advises him to "bear welcome" and to "look like the innocent flower" but be "the serpent under it." She'll do all the rest.

Analysis

Lady Macbeth is one of the most amazing of all Shakespeare's characters, and we can see why in this scene. She dominates. No one else in these early scenes can equal the extent of her ambition, the intensity of her spirit, and the strength of her will. Her prayer to the spirits to make her masculine introduces Shakespeare's examination of gender. Is assassination, like war, the province of men? Are women restricted to nurturing children?

Notice how Shakespeare weaves into her words images of darkness and blood. Duncan will never again see the light of day, a raven will announce his arrival, and, if Lady

Macbeth's prayers are answered, the spirits will make the night "thick" like the darkest "smoke of hell." It will be so dark that "heaven" will be unable to peep through "the blanket of the dark" and try to stop her. Lady Macbeth also prays that her blood, like the night, will be made "thick" so she will have no second (meaning feminine) thoughts about the murder.

Act I, Scene 6

Overview

Duncan arrives at Macbeth's castle with Malcolm, Banquo, Macduff, and others. The king compliments the castle's gentle beauty. Banquo calls attention to the martlets—birds known for nesting in churches—that have chosen the castle for its similar architecture.

When Lady Macbeth welcomes the king and his retinue, King Duncan effusively thanks her for her hospitality. She replies that the Macbeths' humble castle is greatly honored by his presence. Duncan then asks to be taken to the new Thane of Cawdor, whom he loves "highly."

Analysis

Shakespeare is noted for his irony, and we see a perfect example of this in his description of Macbeth's castle. Its description contrasts with what we know is going to happen before the night is over. Even the church-nesting martlets are juxtaposed with the battlement-dwelling ravens previously mentioned by Lady Macbeth.

Act I, Scene 7

Overview

Macbeth is losing his nerve over murdering Duncan. There may be unforeseen consequences. He is Duncan's host, kinsman, and supposedly loyal subject. Furthermore, Duncan has done nothing to warrant an assassination. He is universally admired as a virtuous ruler. The only reason Macbeth has to kill is his own "vaulting ambition." When Lady Macbeth enters the room, he tells her, "We will proceed no further in this business."

That's what he thinks. Outraged, Lady Macbeth calls her husband a coward and says that the only way to prove he is a man is to kill Duncan. She has already devised a plan. While Duncan is asleep, she will get his chamberlains drunk. When they pass out, she will take their daggers. Together, she and Macbeth will slip into the king's bedroom, kill Duncan, spread his blood on the daggers, and place them next to the sleeping chamberlains, blaming them when the murder is discovered. Macbeth is so impressed with his wife's "mettle" that he tells her all her children should be males.

Analysis

The Elizabethans believed that God gave kings their right to rule. To try to kill a king was not just a crime, but also a grievous sin. Loyalty to the king was equated with loyalty to God. Macbeth says he is not afraid of hell, but he doesn't want to become a monster, either. This is his meaning when he says he can do all that "may become a man," but any man "who dares do more is none." If only Macbeth could meet Duncan on a battlefield where killing is done quickly and without thought. He's not cut out for taking someone's life when there's time to think.

Lady Macbeth, however, is definitely up to the task. She doesn't ponder Duncan's virtues, Macbeth's sense of loyalty, or her husband's bravery in battle. She tells Macbeth that he will not be a man until he kills Duncan. By questioning his manhood, Lady Macbeth hits her husband right where it hurts the most. Her statements echo her earlier sentiment, when she asked the spirits to make her a man so she could kill the king without any hesitating feminine thoughts. Now she tells her feminine-thinking husband that, despite knowing the love that comes to a nursing mother, she would rip her nipple from the baby's gums and dash its brains out rather than break a vow as he is threatening to do.

This attack on his masculinity rallies Macbeth to his wife's conviction. He exclaims that all their children should be males, meaning that they all should have the same masculine, warrior-like qualities exhibited by his wife. There's no doubt he means this as a compliment. Her purposes may be sinful, dark, and bloody, but Lady Macbeth is a force unlike any Macbeth has encountered in battle.

Act II, Scene 1

Overview

Banquo and his son Fleance are walking at night in a courtyard of Macbeth's castle. Banquo says that "cursed thoughts" keep him from sleeping. They run into Macbeth, and Banquo tells him King Duncan is asleep. He says he's dreamt of the witches and reminds Macbeth that there

Ian McKellen and Judi Dench as Macbeth and Lady Macbeth

was some truth to their prophecies. Macbeth replies that he has not thought of the witches since they appeared on the heath, but suggests that he and Banquo discuss the prophecies later.

When Banquo and Fleance leave, Macbeth imagines a dagger floating before him. Its handle juts toward him as if inviting him to take hold. The tip of the blade points toward Duncan's room. Macbeth tries to grab the dagger and fails. He wonders if it is real or imaginary. No sooner does he write it off as imagined, however, than blood appears on the blade. Suddenly, a bell tolls. As Macbeth leaves, he says that the sound signifies Duncan's death knell.

Analysis

Macbeth's meeting with Banquo and Fleance reminds us—and Macbeth—of the witches' prophecy that Banquo's descendants will be kings. Macbeth claims he never thinks about them. Nevertheless, he invites Banquo to talk with him later about the prophecies. Why does Macbeth do this? Could he be trying to pretend nothing has happened since the men met the witches? Or might Macbeth have some role for his friend in his new government? Or is it possible that Macbeth might be setting up a meeting so he can kill the only witness to what the witches said? If Macbeth does plan to kill Banquo, his son Fleance will also be a target.

Act II, Scene 2

Overview

Lady Macbeth waits for her husband. The wine that put the chamberlains to sleep has emboldened her, and everything is going according to plan until her husband cries out from within Duncan's chamber. Either he can't find the daggers or the chamberlains have woken up before Macbeth could kill the king. She says she would have killed the king herself if Duncan hadn't reminded her of her own father.

Macbeth returns, his hands covered with blood. He has killed the king. He tells Lady Macbeth that he heard the chamberlains wake up and say their prayers before going back to sleep. He had wanted to say "Amen" with them, but the sight of his "hangman's hands" kept the word in his throat. Macbeth adds that as he killed the king, he heard a voice cry, "Macbeth does murder sleep."

Lady Macbeth tries to calm her husband by telling him that water will "wash this filthy witness" away, but

Anna Netrebko and Zeljko Lucic in Verdi's *Macbeth* at the Metropolitan Opera House

then she realizes that he's still holding the daggers that he was supposed to place near the sleeping chamberlains. When she tells him to finish the job of setting up the chamberlains, he refuses to go back into the bedchamber. He says he cannot bear to look at what he's done. Accusing her husband of being "infirm of purpose," Lady Macbeth grabs the daggers and heads off to where the chamberlains are sleeping.

Analysis

Why did Shakespeare have Duncan die offstage? He knew how much Elizabethans loved killing and bloodshed. He could easily have had Duncan murdered right in front of everybody. Perhaps the reason is a practical one: if the dead Duncan were on stage when Macduff arrived in the next scene, the shock of discovery would not be as powerful.

It might also be that Shakespeare wanted his audience to focus not so much on the murder as on its effect on Macbeth. Macbeth's crime is so horrific that he will never be the same. When Macbeth enters Duncan's chamber, he isn't afraid of hell; when he comes out, he blubbers that he will never again sleep peacefully, and he refuses to go back inside. How can it be that Macbeth—the soldier who led his army into battle against Irish, Norwegians, and Scottish rebels—is afraid to think about one killing and can't bear to see the king's dead body again?

Lady Macbeth tells her husband to wash the blood from his hands while she plants the daggers near the innocent chamberlains. After she's gone, there's a knock at the door. Macbeth notes how "every noise appalls" him. He says that if he were to put his bloody hand—the one that stabbed Duncan—into the sea, it would turn the water red.

Furthermore, Macbeth's hands are not just the hands of an ordinary murderer. They're "hangman's hands." These kinds of hands had an added meaning for Elizabethans. Because hanging was almost as big a spectator sport as plays, the Elizabethans knew that hangmen didn't just string people up and cut them down afterward. They also disemboweled and often cut up the bodies similar to the way Macbeth sliced the rebel Macdonwald. Is this another foreshadowing of Macbeth's own end?

When Lady Macbeth returns to find her husband in the same state as she left him, she points out that her hands are now as red as his, but says she would be ashamed if her heart was also as white as his. In her mind, "A little water clears us of this deed."

At the sound of another knock, Lady Macbeth tells Macbeth to go put on his nightgown and stop worrying. If only he could! If only Duncan could be awakened by the knocks on the door. But it's too late. Having done more than becomes a man, Macbeth no longer is one.

Act II, Scene 3

Overview

A porter, awakened from his sleep, responds to the knocking. Macduff and Lennox, a Scottish nobleman, enter. When Macduff asks what took the porter so long to answer, he's treated to a dissertation on the effects of alcohol.

Macbeth enters, and Macduff asks to see the king. While Macduff is gone, Macbeth and Lennox talk about the nasty weather. Suddenly Macduff returns and cries out that a "sacrilegious murder" has taken place; Duncan's life has been stolen from the "Lord's anointed temple," as his body is called. Macbeth and Lennox run to the king's chamber to see for themselves. A bell rings and everyone comes running. "Confusion," as Macduff had predicted, "hath made his masterpiece!"

Confusion has little effect on Macbeth, however. When in crisis, he doesn't have to think; he only needs to act. He kills the chamberlains, and when Macduff asks why, he says he was overwhelmed by his "violent love" for Duncan. Lady Macbeth faints, but that doesn't slow Macbeth down. While Banquo and Macduff ensure that Lady Macbeth is carried from the room, Macbeth calls a meeting of the nobles to discuss the next action to take. Macbeth has yet to be crowned, but already he's acting like the king. Prince Malcolm and Donalbain, meanwhile, conclude that as Duncan's heirs their lives are in danger and decide to flee: Malcolm goes to England and Donalbain to Ireland.

Analysis

The appearance of the porter provides some relief from the tension of Duncan's murder, but not much. While his lowly station and his conversational tone—as opposed to the iambic pentameter used by the nobles—indicate that he's not very important, the porter's words do contain statements that we immediately recognize as true. The Macbeths' castle at Inverness is no longer the sweet, pleasant nest described earlier by Duncan and Banquo; it's a living hell. For all the confusion that is in Macbeth's mind, he might as well be drunk. He imagines daggers floating in midair, hears voices telling him that he'll never rest peacefully again, and can't remember to leave the incriminating daggers next to the sleeping chamberlains. The porter's final words—"I pray you, remember the porter"—are ironic, since he has referred to himself as the Devil. Macduff's appearance at the door is ironic as well. His knocks, which critics view as death knells, foreshadow his killing of Macbeth.

However, the nasty weather taking place outside is not ironic. It mirrors the dark confusion and bloody turmoil taking place inside. Lennox tells Macbeth that chimneys have blown down, screams of death fill the air, birds are shrieking, and the earth itself is shaking. Macbeth's response, "'Twas a rough night," has been interpreted by some as a sign of his distraction. Because he's thinking of the impending discovery of Duncan's body, he's not really listening to Lennox.

Saying that it is a "rough night" is an understatement. Macduff's use of the word sacrilegious and his description of the murderer as someone who broke open "the Lord's anointed temple" and stole "the life of the building" underscores the Elizabethans' belief in the divine right of kings. Duncan's death is nothing less than an attack on God's preordained governing structure. It's so heinous that no word can describe it: "Tongue nor heart cannot conceive nor name thee!" Macduff exclaims.

No sooner does Macduff announce the murder of Duncan than Macbeth's course of action becomes clear. Becoming once again the nonthinking warrior-hero, he kills the sleeping chamberlains before anyone can question them. Not everyone, however, is convinced of the chamberlains' guilt. When Malcolm asks who murdered his father, Lennox replies that "Those of his chamber, as it seemed, had done it." *Seemed* is the key here. Banquo and Macduff also have their doubts. When the nobles meet, they agree "this most bloody piece of work" should be investigated further, but nothing seems to come from their suspicions—not yet, anyway.

So much action (several battle scenes) and so many deaths (executions, assassinations, and murders) are taking place offstage, we have to raise the question again: Why is Shakespeare depriving his audience of the blood and gore they've come to expect from his plays? Some critics believe that he wants us to focus instead on the witches' prophecies, Macbeth's state of mind, and the chaos that results from Duncan's death. Others suggest that Shakespeare is taking his lead from Greek playwrights, who kept most of their violent scenes offstage. Unlike the Romans and the British, the Greeks wanted their audiences to imagine violent acts through the actors' verbal descriptions. They knew that the scenes that viewers imagined in their minds would have

Murder in the air disturbs the horses.

a more significant impact than any stage representation. Still other critics hold that Shakespeare was trying to please his biggest fan: King James I. James, as everyone in his court knew, didn't like long plays, and *Macbeth*, which Shakespeare wrote in his honor, is one of the playwright's shortest.

Act II, Scene 4

Overview

Ross, a Scottish thane, discusses with an old man the strange natural events that they've recently witnessed. The old man has never seen anything like it: An owl has killed a falcon, and Duncan's horses have gone wild and eaten one another. It's as unnatural as "the deed that's done," the king's murder. Ross agrees. The "heavens," he says, are "troubled with man's act."

When Macduff arrives, Ross asks him who "did this more than bloody deed?" Note the word more. Macduff cautiously answers, "Those that Macbeth hath slain." Ross is not convinced—the chamberlains had nothing to gain. Again, perhaps not sure how much he can trust Ross at this point, Macduff tells him what the nobles have concluded: the chamberlains were bribed by Duncan's sons and, having been found out, the brothers fled Scotland.

The nobles have also named Macbeth king, but Macduff will not attend the coronation. He's heading to his home in Fife instead.

Analysis

The purpose of this scene is to fill us in on the thanes' decision to name Macbeth king and inform us of Macduff's decision to miss the coronation. But Shakespeare is never satisfied with merely providing updates. Every scene is an opportunity to say something more than what is apparent. When Ross describes the "heavens" as being "troubled with man's act" and threatening "his bloody stage," for example, Shakespeare is referring to the underside of the roof that covers the stage. Known as "the heavens," it's decorated with stars and symbolizes the heavens where God resides. Shakespeare is telling his audience through Ross that God is not pleased with what he sees taking place below him, and is letting them know of his displeasure using unnatural events.

Moreover, Macduff's decision to return to his home rather than attend Macbeth's coronation is not just an indication of preference or a sign of fatigue. It is an insult to Macbeth that underscores Macduff's suspicions about who really killed Duncan. It also sets up the final confrontation between Macbeth and Macduff.

Act III, Scene 1

Overview

In the royal castle at Forres, Banquo can't help but think about the witches' prophecy that Macbeth would become king and Fleance would establish the royal lineage for years to come. The first part of the witches' prediction has come true, but Banquo fears that Macbeth has "played most foully" to bring it about. Banquo's thoughts, which hint at his own ambition, are interrupted by the Macbeths and the royal court. The Macbeths invite Banquo to attend the feast they're hosting that night. Banquo accepts their invitation, but says he'll be away most of the day. If his horse is not up to it, he may not be back until after dark.

Banquo leaves, as does the rest of the court, and Macbeth asks a servant to show in the two men who have been waiting to see him. While the servant fetches the men, Macbeth, as Banquo did earlier, reviews the prophecies. If everything they said has so far come true, what reason is there to doubt the rest of their predictions? Did he murder Duncan just so Banquo's son could be king? Is he destined to wear a "fruitless crown"?

The men who have been hired to murder Banquo and Fleance enter, and Macbeth reminds them of a previous conversation. He asks the men if they remember all the wrongs he said were done to them by Banquo. They do. Following his wife's example, Macbeth asks if they are manly enough to take their revenge on Banquo. They are. Will the men promise that, before the night is over, Fleance's soul will join his father's in its search for heaven? They promise that it will.

Analysis

Scotland is quickly becoming an intolerable place to live. Macbeth killed Duncan to become king; he killed the chamberlains to blame the murder on them; now he has to kill Banquo and Fleance to prevent their family from ruling Scotland for generations to come.

And what about Macbeth's motivating the hired murderers with the same challenge to their masculinity that his wife used on him previously? What does all this talk about masculinity say about men? Is testosterone more powerful than friendship, loyalty, common sense, and God's will combined?

And why is Banquo planning to go riding with no destination mentioned on the day of the great banquet? Could he be thinking about following Macduff's lead in boycotting the feast and, at the same time, covering himself if he decides to show up after the party is over?

Act III, Scene 2

Overview

Lady Macbeth has discovered that murder has not brought happiness, or peace. It is better to be "that which we destroy" than "by destruction dwell in doubtful joy." Macbeth couldn't agree more. It would be better if he and Lady Macbeth were with the dead "whom we, to gain our peace, have sent to peace" than torturing themselves with guilt. However, they still decide to murder the two latest threats to the throne: Banquo and Fleance.

In an earlier scene, Lady Macbeth told her husband to "look like the innocent flower" but "be the serpent under it." Now Macbeth tells his wilting flower of a wife that, as long as Banquo lives, they are unsafe. Once again, they must wear faces that disguise their dark hearts.

Analysis

Macbeth talks a good game but, because his head is "full of scorpions," his voice lacks the conviction that Lady Macbeth's had when she persuaded him to murder Duncan.

What about Lady Macbeth? Is this the same woman who spurred her husband on to murder by demeaning his masculinity? Who said that the blood on Macbeth's hands could be washed away with a bit of water? Her tune has

Rene Pape and Moritz Linn in Verdi's *Macbeth* as Banquo and Fleance

changed, too. She soliloquizes that "all's spent, / Where our desire is got without content."

Act III, Scene 3

Overview

Macbeth's murderers, now three in number, ambush Banquo and Fleance on their way back to the castle. Fleance's torch goes out in the struggle, but before Banquo dies, he tells his son to flee.

Analysis

Macbeth's ambition has spun out of control. Will he now have to kill the killers, too? If he does kill them, whom will he hire to murder Fleance? And where did that third murderer come from? There were only two who met with Macbeth earlier in the day. Some critics believe that the unexplained third murderer indicates that there might be lines missing from the original text. Many cite this scene as an example of lines that Shakespeare didn't write. There's nothing in them but plainly stated action.

Act III, Scene 4

Overview

Before the planned banquet begins, Macbeth meets with one of the murderers. Macbeth hails the man as "the best of the cut-throats," but becomes unhinged when he hears that Fleance has escaped. He feels "cribbed, confined," and "bound" to annoying "doubts and fears." Nevertheless, he tells himself to remain calm; "the worm that's fled" has no teeth—yet.

Macbeth returns to the banquet, but finds a guest he hadn't expected: Banquo's ghost. Not only has the ghost shown up uninvited, but he's sitting in Macbeth's chair. Macbeth talks to the ghost, but because he's the only one who can see the spirit, what he says doesn't make much sense to the guests. Ross concludes that Macbeth is not well and suggests that the party break up, but Lady Macbeth tells the nobles to ignore her husband. She explains that he's had these fits since he was a child and that this one will soon pass. Her first words to her husband are almost predictable: "Are you a man?"

What worked well in the past does not work so well now, however. Macbeth cannot get a grip on himself until Banquo's ghost leaves. But when the king raises his glass for a toast to "our dear friend" Banquo, the ghost returns, sending Macbeth once again into babbling that's just clear enough to raise the nobles' suspicions. Afraid that her husband might reveal their roles in the murders of Duncan and Banquo, Lady Macbeth takes Ross up on his earlier suggestion to cut the party short.

Alone with his wife, Macbeth claims that Banquo's ghost is out for blood. He has also learned that Macduff wasn't at the party, a signal that Shakespeare's audience would immediately recognize as treasonous. Before taking any action, however, Macbeth decides to talk again with the witches.

Analysis

What is supposed to be a celebration of Macbeth's ascension to the throne turns into what Macduff predicted in an earlier scene: a masterpiece of confusion. Because Macduff has chosen to excuse himself from the banquet, Macbeth has a pretty good idea where his next challenge will come from and who his next target will be. But Macduff is only the latest person to reach the top of Macbeth's hit list. There's still the heir, Malcolm, in England and his brother, Donalbain, in Ireland. They have yet to develop the "venom" they need to kill, but they will. Not that it matters to Macbeth. He says he's already so steeped in blood that to wade through any more would only make his return from the monster he's become to the human he once was as "tedious" as the dark journey that has brought him to this point.

This brings us to Banquo. Why did Shakespeare choose to have Banquo's ghost appear and not Duncan's? In *Holinshed's Chronicles*, Shakespeare's source for the play,

A ghostly guest at the Macbeths' feast

Banquo is Macbeth's accomplice in the murder of Duncan. But in Shakespeare's version, he's an example of a man who, unlike Macbeth, can keep his ambition in check and whose descendants will establish a royal lineage for generations to come: right down to King James I. Critics who read *Macbeth* in terms of its historical context suggest that Shakespeare presented Banquo in a positive light because he wanted to honor King James and keep those requests for royal performances coming.

Act III, Scene 5

Overview

On the heath, the witches meet with Hecate, goddess of witchcraft. She admonishes them for messing with Macbeth's life without first consulting her. She tells the witches that she's in charge from now on, and instructs them to create illusions that will confuse Macbeth and lure him into a false sense of security, which Hecate says is "mortals' chiefest enemy."

Analysis

This time Hecate appears in a scene with the witches. Why? Did Shakespeare really need to include this scene in his play? If we need to know the witches' reasoning behind their actions in the opening scene of the next act, then the answer is yes. The answer is also yes if you believe that Shakespeare wanted to engage James I's interest. Eliminating all but one of the visual representations of Macbeth's murders allows Shakespeare to emphasize the supernatural elements in his play. Witches, ghosts, and imagined flying daggers focus our attention on the moral decay and confusion of Macbeth's dark thoughts as well as his bloody reign.

Act III, Scene 6

Overview

Lennox and a lord discuss the state of Scotland. It's not a pretty picture. They know that the "tyrant" Macbeth is responsible for the murders of Duncan and Banquo, and

The witches foretell Macbeth's fate.

the lord tells Lennox that Macduff has joined Duncan's son Malcolm in England to seek military help at the court of King Edward.

Analysis

By including in his play the information that Malcolm and Macduff are seeking the aid of King Edward the Confessor, Shakespeare honors the bond of cooperation and mutual interest that has united England and Scotland for centuries. Thus, it becomes clear to the audience watching the play that Macbeth's murders involve not only Scotland but the larger world as well. If nature is to be restored and the political chaos in Great Britain eliminated, Macbeth has to go.

Act IV, Scene 1

Overview

Macbeth meets the Weird Sisters around a boiling cauldron and demands to know his fate. In response, the witches create frightening and confusing apparitions: the disembodied head of a warrior that warns Macbeth to beware of Macduff (Macbeth already knows that Macduff is his enemy), a bloody child who tells Macbeth that "none of woman born" shall harm him (Macbeth is relieved to hear this, but vows to kill Macduff anyway), and a crowned child holding the branch from a tree who tells Macbeth that he won't be vanquished until Birnam Wood moves to Dunsinane Hill (Macbeth is reassured as this must be impossible).

As helpful as he thinks all these prophecies are, however, Macbeth has one more question: Will Banquo's descendants reign? A line of eight kings appears, with the last holding a mirror; the kings are followed by Banquo's ghost. The witches disappear, and Lennox enters to inform Macbeth that Macduff has fled to England. Without a second thought, Macbeth resolves to kill Macduff's wife and children at their home.

Analysis

Who are the Weird Sisters? Their name comes from the Anglo-Saxon word wyrd, which means "fate," but are the witches' prophecies fate? They are a powerful trinity, but how much control do they actually have over what happens? These are difficult questions to answer. Everything they predict comes true, but can they cause their predictions to come true? They know how to torment Macbeth, for example, but they don't seem to be able to harm him anymore than they could harm the sailor's wife who refused to share her chestnuts. Ironically, the witches, who come from the direction of hell if they enter the stage through its trap door, pose a theological question that the Elizabethans were familiar with and that many Christians still debate today: If God is all-knowing, then he knows everything that is going to happen. If he knows everything that is going to happen, then the future is already determined. If the future is predetermined, then people have no free will. If people have no free will, then they are not responsible for their actions. Nevertheless, God holds them responsible. Is that fair? Shakespeare seems to address this paradox through the witches. They, like God, can see into the future, but their seeing into the future does not determine how Macbeth or Banquo will act. Banquo, like Macbeth, is ambitious, but he doesn't act

Lily Hudson as Lady Macduff in a Native American version of *Macbeth*

on his ambition. He knows the boundaries placed on him by God. Macbeth, on the other hand, knows that murder is criminal and sinful, but kills anyway.

The prophecies provide Macbeth with the false sense of confidence that Hecate desired, but because we know that he is being deceived, we see the apparitions as signs that foreshadow the way the prophecies will be fulfilled. While Macbeth takes the witches literally, we can only wonder how Shakespeare is going to make Birnam Wood come to Dunsinane. We know Macduff is going to end Macbeth's bloody reign, but how can he do it if he is not "of woman born"?

As for those eight kings lined up "to the crack of doom," some of them carry the three balls and two scepters that make up part of the royal insignia of Great Britain.

The realization of this prophecy is reinforced by the king who carries the mirror. He not only creates, through its reflection, an infinite number of descendants from Banquo, but he can also reflect in the mirror the image of James I sitting in the audience.

Act IV, Scene 2

Overview

At her castle in Fife, Lady Macduff demands an explanation. She wants Ross to tell her why her husband has fled to England. Ross says that it isn't clear that he fled and begs her to have patience. She refuses. Her husband, she says, is a coward and a traitor who doesn't love his family. When Ross leaves, she tells her son that his father is dead, but the boy argues wittily and convincingly that he is not. Their clever repartee wins the audience's affection and, when a messenger interrupts them and tells them to flee for their lives, they win the audience's sympathy as well. After claiming that she has done no harm and, consequently, has no reason to flee, Lady Macduff immediately regrets her "womanly defense." That she has done no wrong is irrelevant. Macbeth wants her and her son dead. When the murderers enter, one of them calls Macduff a traitor. The boy calls the murderer a villain and a liar, but pays for his bravery with his life. Lady Macduff flees the room, with the murderers in pursuit.

Analysis

Unlike Macbeth's earlier murders, which were committed to gain or retain power, no amount of reason can justify these killings. In other words, Macbeth has murdered simply to cause harm. According to his own definition, he is no longer a man but the monster he feared he would become if he murdered Duncan.

Act IV, Scene 3

Overview

Outside King Edward's palace in London, Macduff offers his services to Malcolm, but Malcolm says he doesn't trust the noble thane. He accuses Macduff of being Macbeth's ally and leaving his wife and children in Scotland, knowing that the tyrant wouldn't harm them. When Macduff refutes these charges and encourages Malcolm to fight for his rightful throne, Malcolm replies that, as bad as Macbeth is, he, Malcolm, would be an even worse ruler. He then lists many reasons why he would make "black" Macbeth "seem as pure as snow." Finally, Macduff can't take it anymore. He tells Malcolm that he is not fit to live, let alone govern Scotland. Malcolm then admits that he's been testing Macduff and now, convinced of Macduff's loyalty, is ready to place himself under the older and wiser man's guidance.

Ross arrives from Scotland. After first telling Macduff that his wife and children are well, he breaks down and admits that they have been murdered. Malcolm, again displaying the youth and inexperience he revealed through his absurd test of Macduff's loyalty, encourages the thane to take the news of his family's fate like a man. Macduff says he will, but first he must "feel it as a man."

Analysis

Once again, Shakespeare asks us to consider what it means to be a man. The immature Malcolm associates manhood with a warrior's skills and attitudes, but the wiser Macduff tells him that there's more to being a man than aggression and killing. It's also important to feel pain, grief, and loss. This is advice that Malcolm needs to heed if he hopes to be a successful ruler of Scotland.

Act V, Scene 1

Overview

A doctor and a gentlewoman discuss Lady Macbeth's new habit of sleepwalking. Lady Macbeth suddenly appears carrying a candle. She imagines that there's blood on her hands and no amount of washing will remove it. She says, "Out, damned spot! Out, I say!" But there's too much blood for any amount of water to remove. "Who would have thought the old man to have had so much blood in him?" she asks herself. This is a dramatic change from her earlier cold ruthlessness.

The doctor comments that Lady Macbeth's disease is "beyond my practice," and the gentlewoman notes that she would not "have such a heart in my bosom for the dignity of the whole body." In short, Lady Macbeth is beyond hope. Guilt and paranoia have killed her as assuredly as the chamberlains' daggers sent Duncan to his final rest. Her immediate recourse is to go to bed. Her final words are "What's done cannot be undone."

Wracked with guilt, Lady Macbeth spends her nights sleepwalking through the castle.

Analysis

The action is going to come rapidly to a close now. Instead of the longer preparatory scenes of the previous acts, a series of short scenes will lead to Macbeth's inevitable end. What holds our interest from here on out is discovering how the prophecies will be fulfilled, how Macbeth will die, and what will happen to Lady Macbeth.

Act V, Scene 2

Overview

As the rebellious Scottish lords gather their forces to meet Malcolm and his army, they report that Macbeth has fortified Dunsinane Castle for a siege.

Analysis

This scene shows that the country's revulsion at Macbeth's crimes has caused many forces to unite against him.

Act V, Scene 3

Overview

Macbeth confidently dismisses reports that a large army is preparing to besiege his castle. As long as Birnam Wood remains in Dunsinane, he is safe. And isn't their leader, Malcolm, born of a woman? Defeat and death are impossible. But Lady Macbeth's descent into madness is not. When Macbeth asks the doctor if he cannot "minister to a mind diseased," he learns that the only person who can help Lady Macbeth is herself.

Analysis

Remember the witch goddess Hecate telling us that security is mortals' biggest enemy? How right she was! Recall all that talk about how much better it is to have action done quickly. If only the Macbeths had taken the time to consider carefully the full consequences of their behavior. Now what's done cannot be undone; their fates are sealed.

Act V, Scene 4

Overview

Malcolm orders his soldiers to cut down branches from the trees in Birnam Wood and carry them to camouflage the size of his army as it marches toward Macbeth's castle at Dunsinane Hill.

The hills of Dunsinane, the site of the battle between Malcolm and Macbeth

Analysis

The witches prophesied that Macbeth would not be defeated until Birnam Wood came to Dunsinane Hill. Those now-famous trees are about to make their trip. The "confident tyrant," as army commander Lord Siward notes, is in for a surprise.

Act V, Scene 5

Overview

Macbeth, wearing armor that he doesn't yet need, orders banners to be flown from his castle and boasts of his coming victory. But the bloodcurdling sound of women crying interrupts his reverie: Lady Macbeth has died. Shocked by his loss, Macbeth famously reflects on the meaninglessness of life. Life is, he says, "a tale / Told by an idiot, full of sound and fury, / Signifying nothing."

More bad news follows: The trees of Birnam Wood have arrived at Dunsinane. Macbeth replies that he's beginning to grow "a-weary of the sun," but he vows to go down fighting.

Analysis

Lady Macbeth has died, but how? Is it logical to assume that, given her psychological state, she has killed herself? Yes. Is this a conclusion that Macbeth could reasonably reach? Yes. Is it something the audience might assume? Again, the answer is yes, but it is not stated explicitly in the text.

We don't like Macbeth, but it's hard not to admire his courage. Though he's become a monster, he will die like a man.

MALCOLM'S VOW.

Page 44.

Malcolm vows to be a worthy ruler.

Act V, Scenes 6 and 7

Overview

Malcolm orders his soldiers to throw down their branches and mount their attack under the leadership of Macduff. In the midst of battle, Macbeth—confident that "none of woman born" shall harm him—is a killing machine. One of his victims is Lord Siward's son. Elsewhere on the battlefield, Macduff searches for Macbeth. If he can't personally avenge the murder of his wife and children, their ghosts will haunt him for the rest of his life. Malcolm and Lord Siward, meanwhile, prepare to enter Macbeth's castle.

Analysis

Whatever deaths Shakespeare may have kept his audience from viewing—those of Macdonwald, Cawdor, Duncan, his two chamberlains, Lady Macduff, and Lady Macbeth—he makes up for in these last few scenes. Since most of the previous deaths took place offstage, there's no danger that the battle will seem anticlimactic.

Act V, Scene 8

Overview

Macbeth realizes that he has lost but refuses to "play the Roman fool" and die upon his own sword. As long as his enemies are standing, he will keep slashing. Finally, Macduff catches up with Macbeth. Because he can't be killed by "one of woman born," Macbeth tells Macduff to fight those carrying "vulnerable crests." Macduff, however, has news for the tyrant: He "was from his mother's womb/

Macbeth and Macduff fight to the death.

Untimely ripped." Macbeth realizes that all the prophecies have now come true, but, as he has vowed in an earlier scene, he dies fighting.

Analysis

We don't have much compassion for Macbeth. In fact, his death is something of a relief after all the bloodshed he caused. But we also can't help but admire his courage at the end and regret how it is a waste. His character is not without some sympathy. He realizes that his isn't a "charmed life." All the impossible prophecies have come true, his kingdom is in ruins, his wife is dead, and his time on earth is nearly over, yet he'd rather die fighting than suffer the public humiliation of kissing "the ground before young Malcolm's feet" and being "baited with the rabble's curse."

Act V, Scene 9

Overview

Lord Siward learns that his son died with his wounds on his chest, and Malcolm shows that he has learned a lesson about manhood from Macduff when he expresses his sorrow for the lost soldier. Macduff enters with Macbeth's head on a pole, and Malcolm invites all his loyal followers to his coronation.

Some texts do not introduce a new scene here, but instead have Macbeth and Macduff fight to the death onstage, with Macduff carrying Macbeth's body offstage before the arrival of the victorious forces.

Shakespeare's Malcolm is based on the historical King Malcolm III.

Analysis

Malcolm reveals his suspicion that Lady Macbeth took her own life. As the rightful heir to the Scottish throne, Malcolm sets the final tone of peace by promising that the disruption in the natural order that Macbeth has caused will be remedied in good time.

Analysis of Major Characters

Macbeth

Macbeth's reputation as a warrior precedes his entrance on the stage. Brave, noble, successful in battle, and respected for his leadership, there is much to admire in him. We soon discover, however, that he is also superstitious and ambitious. Left to his own devices, Macbeth might not have acted on his ambition. But when he hears the witches' prophecy that he will be king, Macbeth doesn't know if he wants to wait for the crown to come to him. He may even have already been entertaining thoughts about murdering the virtuous, aged king.

Macbeth's ambitious thoughts turn quickly into action after Lady Macbeth questions his manhood, but he doesn't rush off to kill Duncan with the same intensity that he used to slay his king's enemies. He has reservations about killing someone who has been good to him, a leader who is much admired by the Scottish people. Three times he hesitates to murder Duncan; he even refuses outright at one point. The reasons for Macbeth's hesitation are partly what prevent him from becoming one-dimensionally evil and allow us to sympathize with him to some degree, especially when we see how tormented he is by guilt and remorse. What keeps our sympathy in check, however, is Macbeth's lack of repentance—this and his continued bloodshed.

In addition to having a conscience, Macbeth has an active imagination. He sees flying daggers pointing the way to murder, oceans of blood that cannot be washed from his hands, and the ghost of one of his victims, which is as real to him as any living being. These hallucinations

Peter O'Toole as Macbeth in 1980

as well as his conscience have such a tight hold on him that he can find relief from their torment only in action. In short, Macbeth is capable of the most horrendous violence—the murders of Lady Macduff and her children are an example—as long as he doesn't think about the consequences of what he does. Conversely, he hesitates to kill King Duncan because he pauses to think beyond the crime he plans to commit. Unfortunately for his victims, Macbeth's guilt and remorse are never so torturous as to prevent him from taking innocent lives.

When Macbeth hears the news of his wife's death, he is plunged into despair at the realization of what their ambition has wrought. Life without Lady Macbeth—and their love for one another is unquestionable— has no meaning. Macbeth expresses this pessimism in what is perhaps the most famous speech in the play:

> ***Life's but a walking shadow, a poor player***
> ***That struts and frets his hour upon the stage***
> ***And then is heard no more; it is a tale***
> ***Told by an idiot, full of sound and fury,***
> ***Signifying nothing.***
> *(V. 5.)*

If only guilt, remorse, and pessimism were enough to make Macbeth admit defeat. But the word *defeat* simply isn't in his vocabulary. His mind may be "full of scorpions," he may not be able to sleep at night, and his murders may have left him increasingly isolated from the Scottish community, but his ambition to reign, his love of power, and his contempt for anyone that "first cries, 'Hold, enough,'" spur him to oblivion. Tragically—some even say heroically—he dies fighting for his life.

Lady Macbeth

Like her husband, Lady Macbeth is proud, courageous, and ambitious. But she's also ruthless. If she does have a conscience, she doesn't let it get in the way of whatever she wants to accomplish, at least at the beginning of the play. She even goes so far as to ask the spirits to "unsex" her so she can kill King Duncan herself and not have to rely on her husband. The spirits can't help Lady Macbeth, however, and she's forced to use traditional "feminine" methods to manipulate Macbeth into carrying out her will. When he resists her proposal to murder the king, she calls him the worst name anyone could call a soldier: coward. Then she taunts him with the suggestion that he is not a man and is not capable of becoming one until he kills Duncan. Any man who is secure in his masculinity,

Derbhie Crotty at the Royal Shakespeare Company Swan Theatre as Lady Macbeth

of course, would not be swayed by these arguments, but Macbeth cannot resist them because, like his wife, he associates manhood with violence and killing.

The strength of Lady Macbeth's will dominates almost every scene in which she appears. She compels her husband to kill Duncan, she calms his nerves after the dark deed is done, and she plants the bloody daggers on the innocent chamberlains. When Macbeth sees Banquo's ghost sitting in his chair at the royal banquet, it's Lady Macbeth who comes to his rescue. She explains to the nobles that her husband's behavior is an illness that has plagued him since childhood, cuts short his inadvertent revelation of the role he and she played in Duncan's murder, and sends her guests home before their suspicions can be roused any further. Even when she realizes the terrible consequences of their murders, she stays her course. She helps Macbeth but doesn't ask for his help; she listens to his complaints, but makes none of her own; and she appears to die by her own hand, rather than someone else's. Yet, like Macbeth, she also has her sympathetic side: She loves her husband, she can't stab Duncan herself because he reminds her of her father, she's tormented by the consequences of their deed, she is sickened at the thought of further killing, and her guilt is so great that it drives her to madness and, eventually, death. At the same time, like her husband, she never repents.

Banquo

Banquo invites comparison with Macbeth. Also brave in battle, he praises Macbeth to Duncan even though the king didn't bestow upon him any rewards for his loyalty and valor. Almost as ambitious but not nearly so superstitious as

Macbeth, he doesn't put too much weight on the witches' prophecies until he sees the effect they've had on his friend and comrade-in-arms. He warns Macbeth that "honest trifles" can betray deeper consequences, but he is in no hurry to discuss their futures, even after the first part of the witches' prophecies comes true. It's not until he and his son Fleance walk late at night through Macbeth's castle that his mood seems to darken. He complains that "cursed thoughts" have kept him from sleeping. Is he thinking about the witches? Probably. Does he think Macbeth may be plotting to kill King Duncan? Possibly. We can't say for sure, but when Macbeth says he killed the chamberlains out of "violent love" for his king, Banquo has his doubts. He's the one who suggests to Macduff that the nobles should meet to "question this most bloody piece of work."

Banquo is traditionally seen as one of the good guys in *Macbeth*, but he's not free of human frailty. Even though he's the only one besides Lady Macbeth to know of the prophecies, he doesn't discuss them with anyone after Duncan is killed. Nor does he take issue with the official view that Duncan's sons committed the murder. And, unlike Macduff, he attends the royal banquet celebrating Macbeth's accession to the throne. In other words, he keeps his ambition in check by not acting on it, but he does nothing to impede the progress of the witches' prophecies, either.

Macduff

Macduff is the model thane. Although he enters the play after the other major characters, he stands morally apart from and above them. It is Macduff whose four knocks on the door after Duncan has been murdered are often said to be death knells for Macbeth. It is Macduff who discovers

Duncan's body and places the murder in the context of the king's divine right to rule. It is Macduff who, because he doubts Macbeth's innocence, boycotts the royal banquet. It is Macduff who counsels Malcolm on what it means to be a man. And it is Macduff to whom Shakespeare gives the honor of slaying the hated tyrant. In short, Macduff is the ideal warrior-hero and can always be counted on to feel with compassion and to do what's right.

He does make one costly mistake, however: leaving his family alone while he meets with Malcolm in London. Macbeth's senseless slaughter of Macduff's wife and children extends the tyrant's cruelty beyond comprehension. There can be no sympathy for him now.

Lady Macduff, who contrasts with Lady Macbeth, is neither ambitious nor political. All she cares about is her family. Her anger at her husband's heading off to London, for example, does not include any consideration of what he obviously sees as a responsibility. Macduff's decision to leave his family was certainly a poor choice, but it wasn't an immoral one. In the end, he fulfills his duty to Malcolm and Scotland and avenges the deaths of his wife and children.

The Weird Sisters

We don't know much about these characters. Some critics say they refer to the three Fates of classical or Norse mythology—the Anglo-Saxon word for "fate" is *wyrd*—but the relation they bear to these spirits is in name only. Some critics say they help create the supernatural atmosphere that permeates the play, others say that they represent Macbeth's unconscious thoughts, and still others say

Macbeth and the Weird Sisters

Macbeth and Power

POWER IS COMPLICATED. We've all heard the old saying that "absolute power corrupts absolutely." Shakespeare was fascinated by the study of power, or at least that's what his plays suggest. Through his characters we see that monsters are very rarely born; rather, they are created. In fact, the play has often been used to examine power relations in our modern world. Adaptations often use settings such as crime organizations, politics, or business, because these are our new battlefields, where people fight for power, respect, and resources.

Films such as *Joe Macbeth* (1955), *Men of Respect* (1991), and *Macbeth on the Estate* (1997) use Shakespeare's classic plot to explore mafia rituals, the relationship between violence and male identity, and power struggles.

The BBC's classic *ShakespeaRe-Told* series recast *Macbeth* in the business setting of a Michelin-starred restaurant, where sous-chef Joe Macbeth initially only wanted for his work to be recognized and respected. It is the arrogance and incompetence of his head chef Duncan and Duncan's son Malcolm that eventually drives him to kill Duncan. Yet it all begins with a talented man who just wishes for respect from his employer.

In fact, Shakespeare's work lies so close to the heart of human nature that in some instances it has even been banned! The 2012 Thai film *Shakespeare Must Die* follows a theater group staging a production of *Macbeth*. It is set in a fictional country that closely resembles Thailand. One of the main characters is a dictator named Dear Leader, who bears a similarity to former Thai leader Thaksin Shinawatra. It was banned by the Thai government due to its anti-monarchy overtones. Director Ing Kanjanavanit pointed to the film's universality: "When Cambodians watch this they'll think it's Hun Sen. When Libyans watch it they would think it's Gaddafi."

that they're just a bunch of loonies who have been made noteworthy by Macbeth's superstitious beliefs. Whatever we might conclude, critics agree that the witches' influence on the play and on Macbeth is considerable.

To begin with, the witches can predict the future. Macbeth is named Thane of Cawdor, he does become King of Scotland, Birnam Wood does come to Dunsinane, Banquo's descendants do inherit the throne, and Macbeth is slain by someone not of woman born. But can the witches control the future? It's unlikely that Macbeth would have killed Duncan if the sisters hadn't predicted that he would be king, but the witches didn't force him to commit the murder. Had he been as patient as he was ambitious, Macbeth would probably have assumed the throne when Duncan died of natural causes. The king may have been virtuous, but he was also old. Of course, if that had happened, there wouldn't have been a *Macbeth*.

When Macbeth sees the witches after murdering Duncan and Banquo, he's a changed man. At their first meeting, Macbeth was brave and honorable—if a little too ambitious for his own good—and he knew the difference between right and wrong. He still knows the difference between right and wrong, but he doesn't care anymore. He hasn't had a moral hesitation since the night he murdered Duncan. In fact, Macbeth has become downright evil. Just to drive home the point of how little influence the witches have had on Macbeth's spiraling descent, Shakespeare has Macbeth commit an act that the sisters are not even aware of: the senseless murder of Macduff's family.

The witches spell disaster for Macbeth, not because they control the future (they don't), but because he believes in their ability to predict it. What he does with the knowledge they provide is up to him. Knowing the future, he also has the power to change it, for good or for bad. The criminal choices he makes are his, and, to his credit, he blames no one but himself. The witches may contribute to the dark and fearful sense of mystery permeating Shakespeare's play, but the tragedy is all Macbeth's.

Chapter Three

A Closer Look

Themes

The Lesson of Unchecked Ambition

The most obvious theme of *Macbeth* is the lesson of unchecked ambition. It's one thing to fight for your king and reap rewards for your valor; it's quite another to kill God's chosen ruler and put yourself in his place. In fact, it's not just a crime but a grievous sin. After hearing that King Duncan has been assassinated, Macduff cries out against this "sacrilegious murder" and claims that "life" has been stolen from the "Lord's anointed temple."

What's interesting about Macbeth's ambition is that, until he meets the witches, he has kept it in check. He *may* have thought about overthrowing Duncan and seizing the crown, but he has done nothing to bring it about. Macbeth might have continued to harbor his fantasies even after his initial meeting with the witches, but he happens to

Macbeth sneaks into Duncan's chamber.

be married to someone much more ambitious. For Lady Macbeth, the question of whether murdering the king is right or wrong is irrelevant. Whatever it takes to secure the crown for her husband is the correct path.

When Macbeth kills Duncan, he unleashes what Macduff calls a masterpiece of confusion. The natural order of the world—the one created by the Elizabethan God—is turned upside-down. The sun fails to shine, animals act in strange ways, and the country is plunged into chaos until the Macbeths' guilt and remorse propel them to madness and their eventual deaths.

Perhaps more interesting than the Macbeths' unchecked ambition is the engine that drives it: love. The Macbeths don't love one another in a particularly romantic way—when Macbeth returns from war, his wife doesn't even welcome him home with a kiss or a hug—but their unwavering support for one another and genuine concern for each other's success and well-being demonstrate that, whatever their courtship romance might have been, their relationship has matured into a partnership in the truest sense. Unfortunately for Scotland, their focus is on power, and the result is murder, madness, and destruction.

The Unsexing of Genders

The Macbeths' marriage presents another theme: what it means to be a man or a woman. The conventional womanly ideal may at first seem to be the apolitical Lady Macduff, who places her family above all other considerations. In this regard, she contrasts with her manly husband, who leaves his wife and children to join forces with the coalition that will overthrow Macbeth. But Lady Macduff is not totally content in her role as housewife and mother. When she's face-to-face with her murderer, she proclaims her innocence instead of picking up a weapon. Immediately, she regrets her "womanly defense."

Lady Macbeth also challenges the conventional definition of what it means to be a woman. She asks the spirits to "unsex" her so she can murder Duncan and not have to depend on her wishy-washy husband. But because she can't keep feminine thoughts from coming between her and murder—the sleeping king reminds her of her father—she's forced to rely on traditional feminine wiles to motivate her husband to do the deed that she would like

Lady Macbeth seizes the daggers.

to do herself. At this, she is a pro. By calling her warrior-hero husband a coward and encouraging a connection in Macbeth's mind between murder and manhood—if he can't kill Duncan he isn't performing like a man—Lady Macbeth equates masculinity and sex with violence and killing. And because Macbeth also associates his image of what it means to be a man with what he would consider masculine forms of action, he finds Lady Macbeth's challenge more motivating than his own considerable ambition.

Later in the play, when guilt has caused Macbeth to imagine that he sees Banquo's ghost, Lady Macbeth tries to help her husband regain some self-control by asking him, "Are you a man?" And in the final scenes of the play, Malcolm tells Macduff to take the murder of his family "like a man." Macduff, whose definition of *manhood* extends beyond that of the Macbeths', answers, "I shall do so, / But I must also feel it as a man."

What Shakespeare seems to be telling us is that sensitivity to others and feeling the pain of loved ones lost has as much to do with being a man as any violence, and though women may sometimes equal men in their desire to take the lives of others, they do not always have the emotional capacity. Women who do transgress in their traditional feminine roles run the risk, like Lady Macbeth, of descending into madness. When Malcolm bemoans the death of Lord Siward's son after the battle to overthrow Macbeth, he shows us that he has learned Macduff's lesson on the importance of sensitivity. Today we would say that Malcolm has gotten in touch with his feminine side. This leads us to believe that his rule as king will be marked by a compassion for others that is as much feminine as it is masculine.

Motifs

The twin symbols of darkness (representing evil) and blood (representing violence) are also major motifs. Almost everything that happens occurs in some dark place: the witches' prophecies on the heath, Banquo's walking around in Macbeth's castle because "cursed thoughts" prevent him from sleeping, Macbeth's sighting of the dagger that invites him to kill the king, the murders of Duncan and

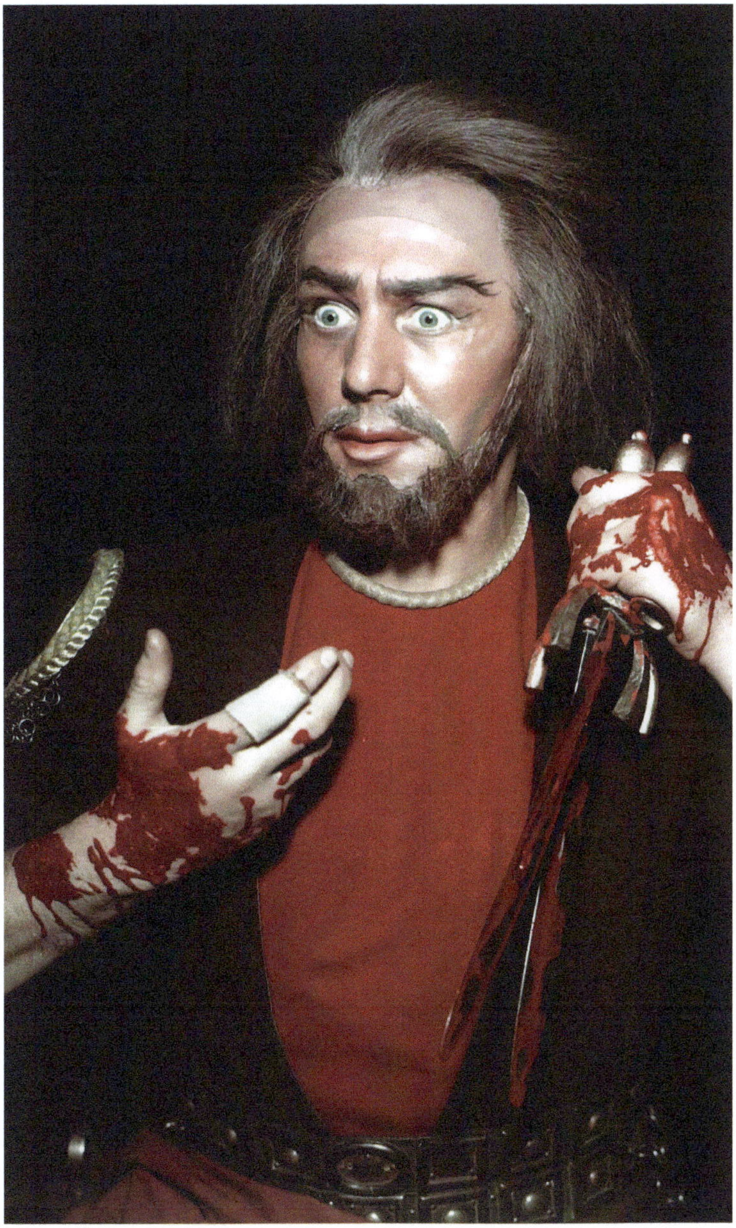

Michael Redgrave as Macbeth in 1947. Macbeth's hands are said to be covered in so much blood that he could turn the sea red if he were to put his hands in it.

the chamberlains in their beds, the attack on Banquo and Fleance, the witches' apparitions in the cavern, Lady Macbeth's sleepwalking, etc. Almost every scene takes place in the dark, at night, or in poorly lit surroundings. Not only are the settings dark, but the language is as well. Macbeth tells the stars to hide their "fires" so light will not see his "black and deep desires." Lady Macbeth asks the spirits to make the night "thick" so she won't have to see the wounds her dagger makes in Duncan's body. Nor does she want anyone in heaven to see her actions and attempt to stop her. The day after Macbeth murders the king, the sun seems strangled, and darkness covers the land.

This is no ordinary darkness. It hides evil as well as any attempt to prevent evil from occurring. Perhaps it is a moral darkness. During her sleepwalking scene, Lady Macbeth insists that light continually be by her side. She thinks it can protect her from the dark thoughts that infest her conscience since the murder of Duncan. Little does she realize that light, which is associated with what is good and right, only makes her more aware of the darkness of her deed. In other words, it illuminates rather than eclipses the blackness in her mind and heart.

On the one occasion when Shakespeare's "traveling lamp" does appear—on the afternoon of Duncan's approach to the Macbeths' castle—it signals that the world is at peace and all is as it should be, if only temporarily. Unaware of the dark plans being made inside, Duncan and his retinue soon discover that they've entered a living hell. The porter who answers Macduff's knocks after Duncan is murdered identifies himself as "Beelzebub" (the devil himself) and the door as "hell-gate." Even Macbeth's valet, whose name is Seyton, is pronounced "Satan."

And then there's the blood. Did evil ever have a more appropriate companion? The word *blood* or one of its derivatives appears in the play more than forty times. The first person to enter the stage after the witches have delivered their opening lines is a soldier wounded in Duncan's battle against the Scottish rebels and their allies. Bleeding from head to toe, he tells King Duncan how Macbeth sliced the rebel Macdonwald from his "nave to the chops," cut off his head, and mounted it on their fortifications. He is no sooner carried from the stage than word arrives of a second battle in which the combatants seemed to "bathe in reeking wounds."

And that's just the beginning! Lady Macbeth asks the spirits to thicken her blood so no feminine thoughts about murdering Duncan will reach her. Later, when tormented by hallucinations of blood that she can't wash from her hands, she asks about the dead king, "Who would have thought the old man to have had so much blood in him?" Even worse off is Macbeth. He's so steeped in blood that if he were to put his hand in the sea, it would turn red.

Macbeth's enemies would agree. Malcolm and Macduff describe Macbeth holding a scepter covered with blood, and Scotland as a bloodstained country that receives a new wound every day. Blood so permeates the words and action of the play that sights and images of it become almost routine. By the time Banquo's murderer shows up at the Macbeths' banquet with the dead thane's blood on his face, we hardly notice. And neither does Macbeth. He even goes so far as to praise the assassin as the "best of the cut-throats" and doesn't so much as flinch when he hears that Banquo's head is wearing twenty wounds as deep as trenches. What goes around, of course, comes around, and the last time we see Macbeth, Macduff has done to the tyrant's head what Macbeth did to Macdonwald's at the beginning of the play.

Symbols

Underscoring the powerful motifs of darkness and blood is Shakespeare's symbolic use of nature. Before King Duncan's murder, nature is the way the Elizabethan God intended. None of the previous deaths mentioned in the play—and there have been many—has disturbed nature because all of the killings were morally justified. The day before Duncan's murder, the sun is shining.

Cawdor Castle in Scotland is often associated with Inverness Castle, where Duncan was murdered.

When the king and his retinue approach the Macbeths' castle, Duncan describes it as having a "pleasant seat." Banquo refers to the "delicate" air surrounding the castle and calls attention to the birds nesting in the castle's "loved mansionry." These birds, called martlets, usually prefer cathedrals. The childless couple inside, of course, is neither the nesting nor the nurturing type. Lady Macbeth tells her husband that she'd rather pull a suckling child from her breast and dash its brains out than go back on a promise like the one he made to kill Duncan. She also asks the spirits to make the air in the castle as thick as the smoke in hell so Duncan can be killed before heaven can stop it.

After Duncan dies, nature quickly turns unnatural. Chimneys are blown down, screams of death fill the air, birds shriek at night, and the earth shakes. Even the sun's light is strangled. Mirroring the guilt-ridden confusion in the murderers' minds as well as the violent chaos soon to be wrought in their kingdom, an owl (which may symbolize Macbeth) eats a falcon (which may represent Duncan), and the dead king's horses break from their stalls and eventually, they eat one another.

So much for the animals and the birds. What about the plants? What symbolic role do they play? Banquo tells Macbeth to "Look into the seeds of time, / And say which grain will grow and which will not." In other words, Macbeth should decide what his future will be, and should not let the witches or anyone else define who he is or what he will become. This is good advice. Duncan tells Macbeth, "I have begun to plant thee, and will labor / To make thee full of growing." The king obviously has big plans in store for his thane. But Macbeth does not blossom as Duncan had hoped. His wife tells him to "look like the innocent flower, / But be the serpent under it." Toward the end of the play, when the Macbeths are reaping the bloody harvest they've sown, Malcolm tells Macduff that Macbeth "is ripe for shaking."

Macbeth, too, describes his end in plant terms. He says toward the end of the play that his way of life has become a "yellow leaf," and that he cannot hope for the harvest that should accompany old age—"honor, love, obedience, troops of friends." His death, which will occur when the branches from Birnam Wood arrive in Dunsinane, is not far off. After Macbeth is defeated, Malcolm announces that Scotland has got to get busy doing that "which would be planted newly with the time." Nature's cycle, which starts in the play with the seeds mentioned by Banquo and ends with the new plantings by Malcolm, is now complete.

One final note: Macbeth dies childless and wifeless, but so does Macduff, who is portrayed as somewhat unnatural because he is not borne by a woman in the usual manner. He's also somewhat supernatural—what today we would call a "superhero"—in that he has no apparent frailties. His loyalty to Scotland, his ability to feel the loss of his family deeply, his advice about the importance of compassion to Malcolm, and his slaying of Macbeth—who, because he has nothing to lose, fights like a "hell-hound"—place Macduff in a supernatural class of his own. Loosely but nonetheless associated with Macduff's supernatural designation are the supernatural Weird Sisters. Their first set of prophecies anticipates the rise of Macbeth, but the second set—complete with a warrior's head, a bloody baby, and a crowned child carrying a branch—announces the coming of the savior Macduff as much as the fall of the evil Macbeth. Without Macduff, Malcolm would still be left in England.

Language

The importance of language in Shakespeare's plays cannot be overemphasized. Any meaningful understanding of *Macbeth* has to include Shakespeare's "poetry" as well as his plot. The thousands of people who flocked to the Globe Theatre to see Shakespeare's plays were not called "spectators." They were an "audience," and, as the word suggests, they came to hear as well as to see. Because there was no scenery, no lighting, and only a few props, Shakespeare had to use his audience's ears to create in their imaginations what could not be physically represented on the stage.

Performances of Shakespeare's plays can be seen at the Globe Theatre in London.

The same is true for us today. To "see" *Macbeth*, we need to recreate the play on a stage in our minds. The words we read cannot just be a series of statements. They must be vivid representations of thoughts that we see. So, when Duncan comments on his approach to Macbeth's castle, "This castle hath a pleasant seat; the air / Nimbly and sweetly recommends itself / Unto our gentle senses" that castle should appear vividly in our mind's eye. Once we discover what happens in that castle, we can appreciate the irony of Shakespeare's exquisite description. In other words, it's Shakespeare's language that prevents *Macbeth* from becoming a relic of the past. It's Shakespeare's language that makes *Macbeth* come alive and continue to live on the imaginative stages of people's minds all over the world.

The people of Shakespeare's time, moreover, didn't shell out their hard-earned pennies to hear actors talk on stage the same way people talked in their homes or at work. They, like their European contemporaries, placed high importance on the beauty and power of words. They even had a name for it: *rhetoric*. Today we think of rhetoric as speech that is insincere or artificial. We might say, for example, that a politician's address to a crowd was "pure rhetoric." This was not the case in Shakespeare's time. For the Elizabethans, rhetoric was the art of persuasion through words.

The key word here is *art*. Shakespeare's characters were expected to say what they wanted to say in words that took ordinary language to a higher level. Their listeners wanted to hear not just *what* was said; they wanted to enjoy and admire the *way* it was being said. Notice how some of Shakespeare's characters refer to the immediate consequences of King Duncan's murder. Ross says that "dark night strangles the traveling lamp" instead of "The sun didn't come out." Macduff announces, "Confusion now hath made his masterpiece" instead of "It can't get much worse than this." When there is no single word to describe an event with the intensity Shakespeare wants to give it, he finds a way for one of his characters to express the feeling better than any single word could accomplish, even if it did exist. "Tongue nor heart cannot conceive nor name thee," Macduff cries out at the thought of what Macbeth has done. Is it any wonder the murderer can't sleep? His head is "full of scorpions."

Even Shakespeare's witches have a way with words. Here are a few lines extracted from one of their soup recipes:

> ***Eye of newt and toe of frog,***
> ***Wool of bat and tongue of dog,***
> ***Adder's fork and blind-worm's sting,***
> ***Lizard's leg and howlet's wing,***
> ***For a charm of powerful trouble,***
> ***Like a hell-broth boil and bubble.***
> ***(IV. 1)***

The words that the witches speak confirm their social position in the audience's mind. In a world where everything conforms to a strict hierarchal order, all the characters in all the plays can be identified and placed in the social order by the ways they speak. Their words are not only enriched beyond what any real person would say, but they often take on added, symbolic values. Take, for example, the witches' "Double, double, toil and trouble, / Fire burn, and cauldron bubble." The lines are clever, fun, possibly scary if you believe in witches, and structured to draw the audience's attention to the messages the witches are about to deliver. The lines are easy to write, easy to say, and easy to listen to. They don't engage our imaginations, however, in the ways that the lines spoken by many of the nobles do. Compare the witches' lines with these from Macbeth:

> ***Will all great Neptune's ocean wash this blood***
> ***Clean from my hand? No; this my hand will rather***
> ***The multitudinous seas incarnadine,***
> ***Making the green one red.***
> ***(II.2.)***

These lines are so highly structured (some would say "elevated") that they almost have to be read twice or even three times, not only to understand what Macbeth is saying but to appreciate the way he is saying it. If he were making a similar statement in today's language, Macbeth might say, "Not all the water in the world can wash away the blood from my hand. I have so much blood on my hand that if I put it in the sea, the sea would turn red." But because he's a nobleman appearing in a Shakespearean play in 1606, Macbeth is expected to speak like someone who is high up in society. His words are what he is.

Read Macbeth's lines again and notice what Shakespeare has created through the words he's chosen to put in his mouth. The first line starts out with Macbeth proclaiming his guilt at having just murdered King Duncan. Can all the water in Neptune's great ocean wash away the blood that's now on his hand? The answer, of course, is a resounding "No." But Shakespeare doesn't stop here. He goes on to say that all the seas of the world will be made "incarnadine." Who but Shakespeare would choose to make an actor utter such a word? The groundlings, those penny-paying spectators in the pit of the Globe Theatre, probably didn't know what it meant, either. But once we discover that *incarnadine* means "to make blood red," we realize that Macbeth's guilt is so great that his hand (*incarnadine* also means "flesh-colored") would turn all the green color of the seas to red.

Now, here's the best part. Do you notice how the "incarnadine" line swells up almost like an ocean wave before receding in the third line? Shakespeare has created an advancing and receding wave in the very lines Macbeth speaks when he is describing the powerful image of a sea turning blood red.

Shakespeare uses language in yet another way. The guilt-ridden Lady Macbeth can't sleep peacefully at night, leading her to sleepwalk through the castle and talk without realizing what she's saying. The words she speaks, however, are not the kind of "elevated" prose that Elizabethans would expect from someone in her noble position. When an actor didn't speak in character, the audience immediately knew that something was wrong. They didn't have to be told that Lady Macbeth—when speaking in a conversational tone of voice as she tried to remove Duncan's imagined blood from her hands—had gone mad. Her sentences, though rambling, are spoken in the ordinary prose of daily conversation:

> ***Out, damned spot! Out, I say! One,—two.—why then, 'tis time to do it. Hell is murky. Fie, my lord, fie, a soldier and afeard? What need we fear who knows it, when none can call our power to account? Yet who would have thought the old man to have had so much blood in him?***
> ***(V.1.)***

When Shakespeare's audience heard Lady Macbeth speaking this way they knew she had lost her mind. Why? Because she wasn't speaking like a noblewoman. By her behavior, the guilt that followed, and the madness that resulted, she has knocked herself out of her social position. Once again, Shakespeare's lines say more than the words they contain. Then, of course, there are the famous speeches. Imagine how Shakespeare's audience must have felt hearing Lady Macbeth utter these words while she waits for Duncan to show up at her castle:

> ***Come, you spirits***
> ***That tend on mortal thoughts, unsex me here,***
> ***And fill me from the crown to the toe top-full***
> ***Of direst cruelty. Make thick my blood.***
> ***Stop up the access and passage to remorse,***
> ***That no compunctious visitings of nature***
> ***Shake my fell purpose, nor keep peace between***
> ***The effect and it. Come to my woman's breasts,***
> ***And take my milk for gall … (I. 5.)***

This speech shows just how determined Lady Macbeth is to seize Duncan's crown for her husband. She wants it so badly that she's ready to kill for it. But there's also something else going on. Lady Macbeth is asking her audience to consider what it means to be a man or a woman. Previously, we heard her husband doubt whether stabbing Duncan is a good idea; now we hear his wife not only praying to the spirits to give her the courage to kill Duncan herself, but associating the act of murder with her own sexual identity. "Unsex me here," she tells the spirits. "Come to my woman's breasts / And take my milk for gall." In other words, Lady Macbeth worries that her feminine instincts, which the breasts and milk represent, are going to stop her from committing the violent murder that men—her husband excepted—don't have to worry about.

To enjoy *Macbeth* beyond the level of plot, we need to use Shakespeare's language to create in our minds a movie of what his Elizabethan audience heard, saw, and understood. We need to read the dialogue as a visual exchange of picture words. In fact, we need to be ready to leap at every verbal image Shakespeare creates. We need to see this baby's brains splattering across the movie screen in our imaginations to appreciate fully how important it is that Macbeth keep his promise to murder Duncan when Lady Macbeth says:

I have given suck, and know
How tender 'tis to love the babe that milks me;
I would, while it was smiling in my face,
Have plucked my nipple from his boneless gums,
And dashed the brains out, had I so sworn as you
Have done to this.
(I. 7.)

Similarly, when the servant informs Macbeth of the English Army's advance, we must "see" through our ears the two characters' fear and desperation:

Macbeth: ***The devil damn thee black,***
thou cream-faced loon!
Where got'st thou that goose look?
Servant: ***There is ten thousand—***
Macbeth: ***Geese, villain?***
Servant: ***Soldiers, sir.***
Macbeth: ***Death of thy soul! Those***
linen cheeks of thine
Are counselors to fear. What soldiers, whey-face?
(V. 3.)

Only when we are able to let our ears be our guide will *Macbeth* be more than something that took place a long time ago in a language we no longer care about.

"Out, out, brief candle!"

Tomorrow, and tomorrow, and tomorrow
Creeps in this petty pace from day to day
To the last syllable of recorded time.
And all our yesterdays have lighted fools
The way to dusty death. Out, out, brief candle!
Life's but a walking shadow, a poor player
That struts and frets his hour upon the stage,
And then is heard no more. It is a tale
Told by an idiot, full of sound and fury,
Signifying nothing.
(V. 5.)

This is the most famous speech in *Macbeth*; it is also the most famous statement of disillusion in the English language. It's so well done that many people believe it to be Shakespeare's own view rather than his tragic hero's.

Macbeth says these words when he learns of Lady Macbeth's death as he prepares for battle against the English. Some critics say that, given how much they loved one another, this passage doesn't express a whole lot of grief. Some say you could take this passage out of the play and no one would notice its absence. It contributes nothing to the plot or to our understanding of Macbeth as a character. Others feel differently. They claim that some pains are so deep as to be beyond words. In this sense, Macbeth's comments on the meaning of life are often said to demonstrate Shakespeare's enormous capacity to understand human nature. Because there are no words to adequately express the sense of loss at his wife's death,

Macbeth doesn't talk about her at all. He chooses instead a subject for which he does have words. And what he says is not unconnected to Lady Macbeth. His words reveal in no uncertain terms the extent to which he has been undone by her death. Life is simply not worth living without her—or perhaps even living at all. It creeps along from day to day: "Tomorrow, and tomorrow, and tomorrow." Note Shakespeare's use of commas. We can't read the words quickly even if we wanted to. He literally makes the line creep tediously. Then there's the alliteration; "petty pace." Can you hear the contemptuousness in Macbeth's voice as he spits out the repeating "p" sound?

And where does this slow, petty, tedious repetition end? In "dusty death." So why not just blow out the candle that is already too brief? Does it matter how long we live? As full of "sound and fury" as Macbeth's life has been, it has amounted to nothing. Is Macbeth's history of murder, madness, and death any less terrible because it signifies nothing? If so, his tale may well be that of an idiot.

It's also a tale told by an actor who "struts and frets" his hour on the stage. Does this mean that the significance we attach to Shakespeare's play is also an illusion? Have we all—playwright, actors, audience—been participating in a reality that, like life, amounts to nothing? You decide.

Interpreting the Play

In *Shakespearean Tragedy: Lectures on Hamlet, Othello, King Lear, and Macbeth* (1904), A. C. Bradley focuses our attention on the main characters in each of Shakespeare's four great tragedies. What he says, basically, is that the central

Austrian physician and founder of psychoanalysis, Sigmund Freud. Many of Freud's philosophies were inspired by Shakespeare's characters.

characters are so intelligent, brave, and strong-willed that only they and their individual tragic flaws could have determined their unhappy ends, not fate or chance. Bradley admits that fate, as represented by the witches, influences Macbeth, but Macbeth is responsible for his behavior and all its consequences.

What's particularly interesting about Bradley's analysis is that he treats Shakespeare's heroes as if they are real people, not just characters. So, when he reads how quickly Macbeth responds to the witches' prophecy that he will be king, Bradley suggests that he had to have already been thinking about killing Duncan.

The next influential critic to come along after Bradley is Sigmund Freud, the famous inventor of psychoanalysis. Because Shakespeare's works are so universally known and admired, Freud often used characters and scenes from them to illustrate his psychological theories. In fact, his idea for the Oedipus complex came to him while watching a performance of *Hamlet*.

For more than eighty years now, Freud's disciples have been analyzing Shakespeare's characters. From their point of view, the supernatural appearances of the witches in *Macbeth* are really the tragic hero's subconscious thoughts. The sisters' first prophecies are a classic example of the kind of wish-fulfillment that we create in dreams. And what about those apparitions that we thought were created by the witches toward the end of the play? They are symbols of the nightmare that rages in Macbeth's mind: his most feared dreams come true in the worst possible ways. Unfortunately for Macbeth, he misreads the symbols.

Because he's not consciously aware of the thoughts that propel his behavior, Macbeth is not totally to blame. Or, at least, he is not without some sympathy. Much of his behavior has been determined by unconscious forces that are not only beyond his control, but of which he isn't even aware.

With the characters covered by Bradley and the Freudians, scholars have had to find other subjects to write about. In Shakespeare's use of images and symbols, they found a literary gold mine. Caroline Spurgeon, in *Shakespeare's Imagery and What It Tells Us* (1935), even goes so far as to create a profile of the character who created the characters: Shakespeare loved the outdoors, was probably good in sports, sympathized with animals, and feared disease.

The best of the image detectors, however, is G. Wilson Knight. He fills seven books with Shakespeare's images and what they mean. These images include animals, birds, sports, blood, disease, medicine, eating, drinking, water, sleeping, family, darkness, light, stars, religion, shelter, seeds, plants, trees, and more. In *Macbeth*, there are more than twenty-five images of clothing alone.

Some of the most interesting of the *Macbeth* images have to do with having children, parenthood, and establishing descendants. The Macbeths don't have any children, Macduff's wife and children are all murdered, Siward's son is slain, Banquo's son escapes death, and Duncan's two sons are spared, with Malcolm set to become the next king of Scotland. Lady Macbeth has had at least one child—she says she knows the joy of a baby suckling at her breast—but we don't know what happened to it. Macbeth is worried that his crown might be "fruitless," and Banquo has been told that his descendants will rule Scotland for generations to come. One of them, King James I, actually sat in Shakespeare's audience. And let's not forget those children who appear as two of the three apparitions the final time Macbeth sees the witches.

Enter the deconstructionists. Generally speaking, the deconstructionists tell us that, in every culture, there is a center of power. The people who are at the power center determine what is important for everyone else in the culture. Those closest to the center are the most important and powerful, and those farthest away are the least. If you landed in the United States from another planet and observed how our society was structured, you might notice that men are more privileged than women, the rich are more privileged than the poor, white people are more privileged than people of color, heterosexuals are more privileged than homosexuals, English speakers are more privileged than non-native speakers, and Christians are more privileged than just about everybody else. In other words, rich, white, heterosexual, Christian men generally control most of the power in this country, and those who look, think, and act like them make up most of the power elite. The powerful may celebrate or at least tolerate the differences that exist away from the center, but they do so only insofar as those who are different don't threaten them.

A similar structure is in place for characters who inhabit the world of *Macbeth*: Because thanes hold most of the power, they are more privileged than any attendants; men are valued more highly than women; war, which is determined by thanes and fought by soldiers, is held in higher esteem than negotiation; and monarchies—God's choice for civic rule—are considered more effective than democracies.

The Evolution of Shakespeare's Characters

MANY CHARACTERS FROM Shakespeare's plays have become modern stereotypes, though their modern meanings don't always resemble their original characters. Modern day Romeos are seen as philandering playboys rather than faithful lovers, while being called a Hamlet probably means you are an obsessive over-thinker rather than a complex and introspective person.

Macbeth has produced such a stereotype with the character of Lady Macbeth. Nowadays, a "Lady Macbeth" is a manipulative woman who stops at nothing to gain power. Despite the fact that feminist scholars have praised the character as an active, empowered female, today's use of the character's name is usually more of a sexist term to describe an ambitious woman.

Yet Lady Macbeth and her husband raise interesting questions about our modern perceptions of gender roles and violence. Is it more shocking if a woman chooses to commit violent acts? One modern parallel is the wildly successful series The Hunger Games. *The Hunger Games* and its sequels are set in a dystopian future where "tributes" from disempowered communities must fight for the entertainment of a privileged upper class. Despite first appearances, there are a surprising number of parallels between the series' leading heroine, Katniss, and Lady Macbeth. Katniss is initially believed

Jennifer Lawrence as Katniss Everdeen in *The Hunger Games*. Like Lady Macbeth, Katniss is a strong female character who must often tell weaker male characters what to do.

to be weak and unlikely to be a threat, mainly due to her gender. However, she quickly adapts to the "kill-or-be-killed" philosophy of the games. She is thrown into a situation where her male partner Peeta struggles with committing the murders required to keep them alive. Much like Macbeth, Peeta is too full of "the milk of human kindness." Gender roles are reversed, and it is Katniss who must take on the traditionally male protective role. Furthermore, Katniss also experiences the trauma of her violent actions, feeling little satisfaction in "winning" after the experience of killing.

Deconstructionists encourage us to break down power centers into their individual parts so their deeper meanings can be understood. Instead of presenting thanes, ladies, monarchs, and attendants as parts of a unified culture, the deconstructionists show us how the Elizabethan world is divided into fragments that are at odds with one another. In other words, each fragment is characterized by its own individual differences, and the people within each fragment either resent, resist, and rebel—or should be—against the forces that restrict them. All, that is, except those who are at the very center of power. They have nothing to rebel against; their job is to keep the existing power structure in place by subduing everybody else. From this perspective, Shakespeare is seen not as an advocate of women's liberation—Lady Macbeth is often praised in feminist circles as an independent-minded, strong-willed woman—but as a supporter of the Elizabethan status quo, with men making the final decisions and women, because of their status and conditioning, having to rely on their wiles to manipulate men into doing their bidding. And that's not all. Reading Shakespeare's plays to fulfill school assignments today is cited by deconstructionists as an example of how the American educational system supports the country's right-wing agenda.

Whether the deconstructionists confirm or challenge your viewpoints of Elizabethan and/or contemporary American culture, to think about *Macbeth* is to become a participant in the creative process that Shakespeare began in 1603. It may be his words on the page, but it's your picture in your mind. How you see that picture, what it means to you, and what about it you believe is significant enough to share with others, are all creative acts. In short, once you've read *Macbeth*, the play not only becomes a part of you, you become a part of it.

CHRONOLOGY

1564 William Shakespeare is born on April 23 in Stratford-upon-Avon, England

1578–1582 Span of Shakespeare's "Lost Years," covering the time between leaving school and marrying Anne Hathaway of Stratford

1582 At age eighteen, Shakespeare marries Anne Hathaway, age twenty-six, on November 28

1583 Susanna Shakespeare, William and Anne's first child, is born in May, six months after the wedding

1584 Birth of twins Hamnet and Judith Shakespeare

1585–1592 Shakespeare leaves his family in Stratford to become an actor and playwright in a London theater company

1587 Public beheading of Mary Queen of Scots

1593–1594 The Bubonic (Black) Plague closes theaters in London

1594–1596 As a leading playwright, Shakespeare creates some of his most popular works, including *A Midsummer Night's Dream* and *Romeo and Juliet*

1596 Hamnet Shakespeare dies in August at age eleven, possibly of plague

1596–1597 *The Merchant of Venice* and *Henry IV, Part One* are most likely written

1599 The Globe Theatre opens

1600 *Julius Caesar* is first performed at the Globe

1600–1601 *Hamlet* is believed to have been written

1601–1602 *Twelfth Night* is probably composed

1603 Queen Elizabeth dies; Scottish king James VI succeeds her and becomes England's James I

1604 Shakespeare pens *Othello*

1605 *Macbeth* is composed

1608–1610 London's theaters are forced to close when the plague returns and kills an estimated thirty-three thousand people

1611 *The Tempest* is written

1613 The Globe Theatre is destroyed by fire

1614 The reopening of the Globe

1616 Shakespeare dies on April 23

1623 Anne Hathaway, Shakespeare's widow, dies; a collection of Shakespeare's plays, known as the First Folio, is published

A SHAKESPEARE GLOSSARY

addition A name or title, such as knight, duke, duchess, king, etc.

affect To like or love; to be attracted to.

approve To prove or confirm.

attend To pay attention.

belike Probably.

beseech To beg or request.

bondman A slave.

bootless Futile; useless; in vain.

broil A battle.

charge Expense, responsibility; to command or accuse.

common A term describing the common people, below nobility.

condition Social rank; quality.

countenance Face; appearance; favor.

cousin A relative.

curious Careful; attentive to detail.

discourse To converse; conversation.

discover To reveal or uncover.

dispatch To speed or hurry; to send; to kill.

doubt To suspect.

entreat To beg or appeal.

envy To hate or resent; hatred; resentment.

ere Before.

eyne Eyes.

fain Gladly.

fare To eat; to prosper.

favor Face, privilege.

fellow A peer or equal.

filial Of a child toward its parent.

fine An end; "in fine" means in sum.

folio A book made up of individually printed sheets, each folded in half to make four pages. Shakespeare's folios contain all of his known plays in addition to other works.

fond Foolish.

fool A darling.

genius A good or evil spirit.

gentle Well-bred; not common.

gentleman One whose labor was done by servants. (Note: to call someone a *gentleman* was not a mere compliment on his manners; it meant that he was above the common people.)

gentles People of quality.

get To beget (a child).

go to "Go on"; "come off it."

go we Let us go.

haply Perhaps.

happily By chance; fortunately.

hard by Nearby.

heavy Sad or serious.

husbandry Thrift; economy.

instant Immediate.

kind One's nature; species.

knave A villain; a poor man.

lady A woman of high social rank. (Note: *lady* was not a synonym for *woman* or *polite woman*; it was not a compliment but simply a word referring to one's actual legal status in society, like *gentleman*.)

leave Permission; "take my leave" means depart (with permission).

lief, lieve "I had as lief" means I would just as soon; I would rather.

like To please; "it likes me not" means it is disagreeable to me.

livery The uniform of a nobleman's servants; emblem.

Lord Chamberlain's Men The company of players Shakespeare joined in London; under James I they became the King's Men.

mark Notice; pay attention.

morrow Morning.

needs Necessarily.

nice Too fussy or fastidious.

owe To own.

passing Very.

peculiar Individual; exclusive.

privy Private; secret.

proper Handsome; one's very own ("his proper son").

protest To insist or declare.

quite Completely.

require Request.

several Different, various.

severally Separately.

sirrah A term used to address social inferiors.

sooth Truth.

state Condition; social rank.

still Always; persistently.

success Result(s).

surfeit Fullness.

touching Concerning; about; as for.

translate To transform.

unfold To disclose.

verse Writing that uses a regular metrical rhythm and is divided from other lines by a space.

villain A low or evil person; originally, a peasant.

voice A vote; consent; approval.

vouchsafe To confide or grant.

vulgar Common.

want To lack.

weeds Clothing.

what ho "Hello, there!"

wherefore Why.

wit Intelligence; sanity.

withal Moreover; nevertheless.

without Outside.

would Wish.

SUGGESTED ESSAY TOPICS

1. How would you characterize the relationship between Macbeth and Lady Macbeth? What do they have in common? What do they see differently? Do you think they love one another? Or is power more important than love?

2. One of the central concerns in *Macbeth* is the examination of gender roles. What does the play say about what it means to be a man and what it means to be a woman? In what ways have gender roles changed for men and women since Elizabethan times? In what ways haven't they changed?

3. What are your thoughts about the witches? What role do they play in *Macbeth*? Do you think they can control the future or just predict it? Is there a difference? Does Macbeth choose his future or is it already predetermined by fate?

4. We hear a lot today about leadership. How would you compare and contrast the leadership styles of Macbeth and Macduff? Are there any ways in which their styles are similar? How about ways in which they are different?

5. The two most prominent motifs in *Macbeth* are the symbols of darkness and blood. Choose one and show how Shakespeare uses it to contribute to our understanding of the play. Does the symbol you've chosen have any particular meaning for any of the characters in the play?

TEST YOUR MEMORY

1. Which of the following lines does Macbeth not say?
   a) "[Life] is a tale told by an idiot, full of sound and fury, / Signifying nothing" b) "Will all great Neptune's ocean wash this blood / Clean from my hand?" c) "Unsex me here" d) "Damned be him that first cries, 'Hold enough!'"

2. Who says the line above that Macbeth doesn't say?
   a) Banquo b) Macduff c) the Weird Sisters d) Lady Macbeth

3. Banquo's ghost attends the Macbeths' banquet because:
   a) he's hungry b) he wants Macbeth to see the evil he's responsible for c) he doesn't want to disappoint Lady Macbeth d) he's waiting for his son's ghost to join him

4. Which of the witches' prophecies doesn't come true?
   a) Macbeth becomes King of Scotland b) Birnam Wood comes to Dunsinane Hill c) Macbeth's descendants become kings d) Macbeth is killed by someone not of woman born

5. Match each quotation below with the person who said it:
   a) Macbeth b) Lady Macbeth c) the Weird Sisters d) Porter

   1) "Thou shalt get kings though thou be none."
   2) "I have no spur to prick the sides of my intent, but only/ Vaulting ambition."
   3) "Out damned spot!"
   4) "This place is too cold for hell."

6. Macduff is not "of woman born" because:
a) he was hatched b) his mother died during childbirth
c) he was delivered by means of a Caesarian section
d) men didn't believe in the equality of women

7. How does Birnam Wood arrive at Dunsinane?
a) as firewood for the winter b) as camouflage for the English Army c) as a coronation gift from Macduff
d) as wood used to make Macbeth's throne

8. How does Lady Macbeth reportedly die?
a) Her husband strangles her for nagging him b) Macduff kills her for abandoning her husband c) Malcolm poisons her for refusing to become his queen d) She commits suicide

9. On the night of Duncan's murder, Macbeth imagines he sees:
a) a dagger floating in the air b) Duncan's ghost saying he won't get away with his crime c) Lady Macbeth packing her bags for England d) his own death

10. Which of the following isn't one of the witches' apparitions?
a) a warrior's head that says, "Macbeth! beware Macduff"
b) a bloody child that says "none of woman born / Shall harm Macbeth" c) a crowned child with a tree in his hands who tells Macbeth he'll never be vanquished until Birnam Wood comes to Dunsinane d) a halo to be worn by Macbeth after he dies and his soul enters heaven

11. What does Lady Macbeth recommend for Macbeth to wash away the blood from his hands?
a) lemon juice b) ginger ale
c) water d) none of the above

12. Why does Macduff kill Macbeth?
a) Macbeth has killed his wife and children b) Macbeth has killed Duncan and Banquo c) Macbeth has become a tyrant d) All of the above

13. What does Macbeth hope to gain by killing Duncan?
a) a castle on Loch Ness b) the crown of Scotland c) peace of mind d) revenge for the king's choosing Banquo as successor

14. Who do the Macbeths blame for the murder of Duncan?
a) Shakespeare b) the drunken porter c) Banquo and his son, Fleance d) the sleeping chamberlains

15. Which best describes Lady Macbeth the last time we see her?
a) She's exhausted from burying all the people she murdered b) She's gone mad with guilt from having helped murder Duncan c) She's angry with her husband's refusal to abdicate the throne d) She's furious with Macbeth for inviting Duncan to dinner

16. What great lesson does Macduff teach Malcolm, the heir to the Scottish throne?
a) Feeling deep pain and loss is not unmanly b) Cutting taxes will keep the people loyal c) There is no problem that can't be overcome by laughter d) He has a lot to learn about women

17. What's the weather like the night King Duncan is murdered?
a) raining as usual b) sunny, a sign of good things to come c) unusually dark and stormy d) foggy, perfect for going unseen at night

18. Why does Fleance and not his father, Banquo, manage to escape from the murderers Macbeth has sent to kill them?
a) Fleance is destined to be king b) Fleance manages to stay on his horse c) Banquo mistakes the murderers for monks d) Fleance fights off his attackers

19. When Macbeth says, "I dare do all that may become a man; / Who dares do more is none," he means:
a) A man can do only so much work before he becomes an animal b) To murder Duncan is to be a man no longer, but a monster c) Ask me no questions and I'll tell you no lies d) Once I kill Duncan and become king, I will no longer be ordinary

20. When Lady Macbeth asks the spirits to "Come to my woman's breasts, / And take my milk for gall," she means:
a) The milk in my breasts has turned to gall because I've never had children b) Turn the milk in my breasts to gall so my child will take milk from his bottle c) Take away from me everything female so I can murder like a man d) Because my husband has the milk of human kindness flowing in his veins, the milk in my breasts has turned to gall

Answer Key

1. b; 2. b; 3. d; 4. a; 5. a; 6. d; 7. c; 8. b; 9. a; 10. c; 11. c; 12. a; 13. d; 14. b; 15. a; 16. b; 17. b; 18. a; 19. c; 20. c.

FURTHER INFORMATION

Books

Macbeth (Folger Shakespeare Library). New York: Washington Square Press, 2003.

Macbeth (Shakespeare Graphic Library). New York: Black Dog and Leventhal, 2006.

Rosen, Michael, and Robert Ingpen. *Shakespeare: His Work and His World*. Cambridge, MA: Candlewick Press, 2006.

Websites

Absolute Shakespeare

www.absoluteshakespeare.com

Absolute Shakespeare is a resource for the Bard's plays, sonnets, and poems and includes summaries, quotes, films, trivia, and more.

Play Shakespeare

www.playshakespeare.com

The Ultimate Free Shakespeare Resource features all the play texts with an online glossary, reviews, a discussion forum, and links to festivals worldwide.

Shakespeare Online: Macbeth

shakespeare-online.com/plays/macbethscenes.html

The entire text of the play, with resources including essays on diverse topics

Film

Macbeth. The Royal Shakespeare Company Production (1978) with Sir Ian McKellen and Dame Judi Dench. Directed by Trevor Nunn.

Audiobook

Macbeth. The Caedmon Recording (1996) with Anthony Quayle and Stanley Holloway.

BIBLIOGRAPHY

Bloom, Harold. *Shakespeare: The Invention of the Human*. New York: Riverhead Books, 1998.

———, ed. *Shakespeare's Macbeth*. New York: Chelsea House, 1987.

Bradley, A. C. *Shakespearean Tragedy: Lectures on Hamlet, Othello, King Lear and Macbeth*. New York: Palgrave Macmillan, 2007.

Bryson, Bill. *Shakespeare: The World as Stage*. New York: HarperCollins, 2007.

Harbage, Alfred. *William Shakespeare: A Reader's Guide*. New York: Octagon Books, 1971.

Hawkes, Terence, ed. *Twentieth-Century Interpretations of Macbeth: A Collection of Critical Essays*. Englewood Cliffs, NJ: Prentice-Hall, 1977.

Holland, Norman. *The Shakespearean Imagination*. New York: Macmillan, 1964.

Knight, G. Wilson. *The Wheel of Fire: Interpretations of Shakespearean Tragedy*. London: Routledge, 2001.

Muir, Kenneth. *Shakespeare's Tragic Sequence*. London: Routledge, 2005.

Shakespeare, William. *The Norton Shakespeare, ed. Stephen Greenblatt*. New York: W.W. Norton, 1977.

Siegel, Paul. *Shakespearean Tragedy and the Elizabethan Compromise*. New York: New York University Press, 1957.

Spurgeon, Caroline F. E. *Shakespeare's Imagery and What It Tells Us*. Cambridge, U.K.: Cambridge University Press, 1935.

INDEX

Page numbers in **boldface** are illustrations.

ABOUT THE AUTHOR

Katie Griffiths is a self-confessed bookaholic and began her love of Shakespeare at an early age. She studied English Literature at University of Edinburgh, where her addictions were further encouraged. She now lives in Hangzhou, China, and teaches English. You can learn more at www.katiegriffiths.org.